Endors

This book, based on Julia's own experience and those of all the women she has helped to raise investment, is an excellent step-by-step guide for any female founder raising investment. It's an easy-to-follow guide with informative real-life case studies, hints and tips and checklists. A must-read!

– Neeta Patel CBE
Former CEO, Centre for Entrepreneurs, NED and Board Adviser

Building on her own experiences building high-growth start-ups, RAISE draws together Julia's passion and expertise to support the female founders of tomorrow with their fund-raising journeys.

Whether you're embarking on your entrepreneurial journey, wondering if investment is the right route for you, or you're a seasoned founder focusing on your fundraising mindset, this book will soon become your 'go-to' guide for all your investment needs.

– Holly Hudson
Community Manager, AllBright

Most books on fundraising are written by someone who raised squillions in Silicon Valley. They inspire, but leave you feeling inadequate and alienated.

We're just not going to follow that trajectory. This book is a breath of fresh air, the personal journey of a founder like you and me.

– Anthony Rose
Founder and CEO, Seed Legals

Mindset to me is everything – and the common-sense way that Julia has broken down the highly valuable, practical, easy-to-follow advice with fantastic real-life case studies will benefit anyone looking to fundraise. The five tiers of having an investible entity – your company, knowing your commercials, communicating in the right ways, connecting and commitment – meet the mark other than the sixth ever-present need for self-confidence.

– Lara Morgan
Entrepreneur, Investor, Mum

RAISE humanises the difficult process of fundraising, but is also filled with practical advice and real insight that will help you work out the best route for your venture. The case studies and checklists make everything that you learn feel actionable and realistic. A must-read for any woman that wants to raise but isn't sure where to start.

– Shanaya Curtis
Senior Equity Fundraising Manager, Crowdcube

Once you get over the injustice, Julia outlines the practical steps of demystifying and addressing the fundraising process, so you can attract investment on your terms. Sadly, I recognise the in-built bias.

This practical handbook highlights how to play the game to your advantage. A must for all female founders.

– John Stapleton
Serial Food and Drink Entrepreneur-turned-Investor

This book is the fundraising bible the female founder community has been waiting for!

It should be in every female entrepreneur's toolkit for success.

– Michelle de Klerk, Founder, The Women's Chapter

RAISE

The Female Founder's Guide to Securing Investment

JULIA ELLIOTT BROWN

RAISE: The Female Founder's Guide to Securing Investment

ISBN: 978-1-7396105-1-7

British Library Cataloguing-in-Publication data

A catalogue record for this book is available from the British Library

Library of Congress Cataloging-in-Publication data

A catalog record for this book is available from the Library of Congress

Cover design: Adam Renvoize

Design: Wayne Kehoe and Andy Meaden

Typeset in Quire Sans Pro by Jim Ford and Monotype

To my sister Katy, who has dared greatly by my side for as long as I can remember, and without whom none of this would be possible

Contents

Foreword

Farah Kabir, Co-founder, HANX

As a former investment banking professional, I'm more at home wrangling spreadsheets than Word docs – but when Julia Elliott Brown asks you to write the foreword for her bible for female founders, you don't say 'No'!

I've long been inspired by Julia's career, and have laid bare my experiences in fundraising for my business, HANX, on her podcast. After reflecting on the highs, lows and everything in-between together, it was clear: we need to do more to demystify the process for all up-and-coming female entrepreneurs.

I'm a first-time founder, having quit my job at Goldman Sachs to partner with my best friend, Sarah, to launch a sexual and intimate wellness challenger brand. With my background in finance and her own in gynaecology, we knew we were perfectly placed to take on the frankly inadequate, outdated (and penis-centric) industry with natural, sustainable products designed for women's bodies.

Like so many founders, we started out with passion and a market opportunity, but not much in the way of practical knowledge. Five years on, we're proudly stocked in more than 2,500 major high-street retailers including Boots, been featured in titles including *Vogue* and *Forbes*, and built a passionate community who share our belief that stigma doesn't belong in our sex lives. It continues to be an exhilarating ride – but as I turn the pages of Julia's brilliant guide today, I can't help but think that our journey would have been much easier if we'd had a copy back then.

As a bright-eyed newbie, you can't help but be seduced by glamorous headlines lauding the successes of Bumble and beyond. Unfortunately, the graft behind the million-dollar raise is something you tend to discover when you're deep in the trenches. In the past five years of pitching to venture capitalists, I've experienced everything from disbelief that women buy condoms to advice to revalue the business – and even getting propositioned.

The fact is, female founders – especially those of us who are of colour – won't have the average journey.

The good news? We're not pursuing that path alone anymore.

RAISE goes behind the bull on LinkedIn to share practical advice and real, relatable stories that properly prepare you for fundraising. From working examples of building cash flow to crafting a narrative around your business, this is less a textbook and more an essential how-to guide. If you don't have a commercial background, it is especially vital.

Most importantly of all, Julia breaks down the importance of mindset. I know only too well that pursuing investment is the mental equivalent of running a marathon. Many don't realise the crucial role of positivity, courage – and especially resilience. It's about time we prioritised our well-being as much as our pitch decks.

Prepare for your copy to become dog-eared, well-thumbed and utterly indispensable.

Introduction

Funding is the number one priority of any growing start-up business, whether you're at idea stage, making early progress and winning customers, or more established and beginning to scale.

But female founders are seriously under-represented when it comes to securing investment. Shockingly, less than 2 per cent[1] of venture funding goes to women-led businesses, and more than half of female founders experience gender bias in the fundraising process.[2]

Over my 25 years in the start-up industry founding, building, scaling and funding high-growth potential start-ups, the dial has barely moved. At the current rate of progress, it will take 100 years before we close the gender funding gap. The global pandemic of 2020 levelled the playing field in some ways, opening up access to investors online and away from the old boys' networks. But in other ways it set women back further, as we struggled to build our businesses and raised investment while also dealing with family life.[3]

Investors stick with what they know, backing businesses and founders with whom they feel more familiar.

How do we, as female founders, crack the fundraising code and unlock the money we need to fuel growth in an investment ecosystem which traditionally has been run by, and for, men?

How do we overcome challenges and inherent bias, and get investors to take us seriously?

How can we make sure that we raise enough money at the right time to build long-term value in our businesses, and make a real difference in the world?

Whether you're just starting a business and want to learn more, or feel you might be ready to raise investment, or perhaps you've tried to secure finance but have come up against challenges, this book will help you navigate your way through and give you the very best chance of flying through your fundraise.

This is not another book written by a guy in a suit from Silicon Valley, or someone lobbing in advice from the sidelines. This guide comes from my own direct experience, having raised serious investment for my own business, and supported hundreds of female founders on that very same journey.

You'll get the lowdown on raising investment from a wide variety of sources, including people in your existing network, professional investors, institutions such as venture capital firms and through crowdfunding, with principles that apply wherever in the world you might be fundraising.

In this book we're going way beyond demystifying the investment ecosystem and technical aspects of raising investment, to cover the whole 360-degree process of fundraising in a step-by-step approach.

You'll learn exactly what investors are looking for:

- How to speak their language, and prepare your financial information and investor pitch.
- How to build your network of high-calibre investors and confidently have meetings with them.
- How to deal with investor questions and gender bias.

- How to negotiate an investment deal that builds real, long-term value for you and your business.

And critically, we'll be looking at mindset and confidence. This is about stepping into your power in a truly authentic way, to unleash your inner 'wonder woman'! Along the way, you'll hear inspiring stories from dozens of female founders who've trodden the fundraising path, sharing their experiences and top tips for success.

Let's kick off with my own fundraising story, so you understand exactly why I'm on a mission to support you with your own fundraising endeavours. The journey to get my own high-growth, start-up business off the ground and raise investment money was without doubt the toughest adventure of my life – out of which came significant learning and, ultimately, great success.

1
My fundraising story

It was early 2009 when my sister Katy and I had the 'lightbulb moment' about our new start-up venture.

Katy was visiting from Hong Kong, where she lived, and we were having a lovely dinner in one of our favourite restaurants in London's Islington. Somewhere between our first course and the main, I looked down at her feet and saw she had the most stunning pair of shoes on: a beautiful, classic pair of pointed high-heel courts in fuchsia suede and snakeskin, with a delicate little bow on the front. Naturally, like any woman would, I asked her: '*Where did you get those shoes?!*'

When she told me she'd designed them herself and had them made specially for her, I could hardly believe it. She went on to tell me the story of how she went to a little backstreet shop in downtown central Hong Kong, filled with shoes of every kind imaginable. She selected the shape and style she wanted, chose her favourite sexy heel shape, browsed through dozens of gorgeous material swatches of every shade and pattern, then picked embellishments to adorn her footwear. The old man in the shop sketched out her design, and within just a few weeks these incredible shoes had been custom-made and were ready for collection, like a dream come true.

By this point, not only was I imagining all these amazing high heels I would design, I was also thinking this would make an incredible online business. From the comfort of their sofas, women all over the world could design their own beautiful, individual shoes to suit them perfectly – we'd make them and deliver them right to their door.

This seemed like such a brilliant yet simple concept: why had this never been done before? I floated the idea past Katy, and her eyes lit up. We poured another glass of vino and started exploring what this business might look like.

At the time I'd been running successful online consumer businesses for 15 years, having been the commercial director at the UK's leading local information website, UpMyStreet.com (which was later sold to Zoopla), as well as establishing my own consultancy business, DigitalSpringboard, supporting a wide variety of brands in commercialising their businesses online. I knew a great deal about e-commerce, marketing, publishing and database design, and enough about technology to see how we could make it possible for customers to design their own shoes on a website.

Katy was working in investment banking, running an operations team across Asia that organised client conferences and events – so she had the production and logistics expertise, plus the geographical advantage to make things happen out in China, where much of the world's footwear is made. Plus she had a strong eye for outstanding customer experience.

The two of us would make the perfect partnership. As sisters, we'd always been close and got on brilliantly, almost like best friends. We both had a similar drive and passion for business, and always wanted to have our own company. As experienced businesswomen and competent leaders, we knew how to bring in the very best expertise in fashion, shoe design and footwear production.

We went home excited, armed with our outline business concept and a vow to get our start-up off the ground. We were clear this wasn't just going to be a back-bedroom business: we wanted to build a brand and company that could scale internationally.

Our ambitions were big: we wanted to revolutionise the way women shopped for shoes.

Funding the beginning

There was a lot to do before we could launch our 'Fashion-Tech' business. The first, and most critical, step was industry and consumer research to flesh out our ideas, sense-check whether our concept had legs, and enable us to develop a full business plan.

Next we created the brand, landing on the name 'Upper Street' to reflect our Islington beginnings, it being the main shopping area there – plus a play on words with the 'upper' of a shoe, and 'street' being both cool and something you walk along – as well as the logo and design assets required.

Then it was on to developing our shoe collection, finding manufacturers, building our innovative and proprietary 3D shoe designer and website, and running our pre-launch press campaign.

It was tricky trying to balance our day jobs, family life and getting this venture off the ground, but somehow we made it work – and it was a lot of fun. We funded everything through our own savings. By the time we launched Upper Street in March 2010, we'd probably spent the best part of £100,000 building our product, technology and brand assets. We were 'all in'.

The business got off to an impressive start. Right from the get-go, we had fantastic press coverage in national glossy magazines, customer orders pinging into our email in-box, rave reviews and strong repeat business – enough to make us feel like we were on to something, and to take the leap into working full-time on our venture.

We continued investing in marketing, pursuing a fast-revenue growth strategy over profitability. Before long, we needed to take on staff to handle customer services and marketing, plus secure office space, so that we could move the business out of my home and offer in-person shoe design appointments. We continued funding the business through our dwindling savings.

The venture capitalists come fishing

About 18 months into the business, following a fantastic double-page spread featuring Upper Street in London's *Evening Standard*, two leading venture capital (VC) firms approached us to talk about investing in the business. Back then I didn't really know much about VC, but the opportunity sounded pretty exciting. I knew that VCs managed funds on behalf of other people and invested in start-ups, but that was about it.

Katy flew over from Hong Kong, and we hopped off to the VCs' big, fancy Mayfair offices in London with heavy glass doors, brass fittings and plush carpets. The venture partners we met wore sharp suits to go with their sharp minds, and they certainly put us through our paces: it was pretty intimidating.

These were 'Series A' VCs, who come in with significant funding when a start-up is ready to scale. Both organisations floated the idea of putting £2–3 million investment into Upper Street, and talked excitedly about how we would need to scale fast and take the brand to the USA, with many other ideas that got us really fired up.

We seriously contemplated taking that vast amount of investment, getting swept along with the glamour of it, thoughts of taking a salary and jetting around the world. But after some reflection, we decided not to pursue the discussions. We simply didn't feel the fit was right at that point: we knew we had a lot more to learn about our customers, and wanted to get our growth strategy much clearer in our own minds before we got on board with the 'big boy' VCs.

But those early conversations opened our eyes to how investment could help us scale more quickly. Profitability wasn't yet in sight, and there was a limit to how much longer we'd be able to fund the business with our own resources. We started to work more seriously on plans to scale the company and understand what funding we would need.

Our first port of call for finance was our business bank. It seemed a good idea to take on debt so we could keep full control of the business for a while longer, and we were confident we could manage the personal risk and the interest payments, so we secured a loan for £150,000.

With enough funding to steer us through for a while and cover our operational overheads, we continued to move our business forward at pace. But we had ambitious plans to open a retail space, grow our team, redesign our website, extend our product lines and put serious marketing budget behind the brand.

We needed a further £500,000, so it was time to get on the fundraising wagon.

The investment trail

After searching online and asking for contact names from all the people I knew, I built a list of early-stage VC firms to approach. By hook or by crook, I got meetings with quite a few of them. The investors I met were all men, which presented me with quite a challenge: they weren't familiar with the fashion or footwear industry, and struggled to understand why design-your-own shoes for women had so much potential.

Every question seemed to have me on the back foot:

> *Do women really buy that many shoes?*
>
> *How would you deal with competition from established shoe brands?*
>
> *Isn't this just a nice little lifestyle company you can run to fit in around your kids and family life?*

It all felt quite insulting.

To top it all, each investor had differing ideas about what we should do with the business – pricing, go-to-market strategy, product lines, technology – purporting to be experts and often talking down to me, even though I wasn't entirely sure their backgrounds and experience really gave weight to their opinions.

I felt utterly confused and unsure, and often came away from those interactions with my energy depleted and confidence chipped. And it was never a straight rejection, just a universal response of: 'Come back and see us when you've made more progress.'

Clearly, they weren't convinced yet – I had more to do to join the dots.

If the VCs weren't biting, I would give these 'angel investors' I'd heard of a try: wealthy individuals who put some of their disposable cash into start-ups. I went to lots of angel pitch events, where each time I presented the business to a room full of (mostly) men in suits. There was so much preparation involved, and it was very stressful and exposing to stand up in front of everyone to be publicly grilled – and nothing much came of it.

In desperation, I engaged an introducer to connect us to his wealthy investor contacts. All of them bar none turned out to be men, and none of them really got it. It felt like we were from different planets, speaking a totally different language.

Six months on (and what felt like sixty million investor meetings later), in September 2013 we were very close to running out of cash. I closed our Islington office, and moved the business back into the spare room at my house to reduce our overheads. Our small but loyal team voluntarily took pay cuts, so we could make ends meet – but it was a sticking plaster. If I didn't raise this money, I would have to shut the doors on the business. The stress was unbelievable: I wasn't sleeping or looking after my own well-being, and my hair was literally falling out.

But revenues were still growing, and I felt more confident than ever that this business could get to the moon; it was just a question of finding the right backers who wanted to get on board our rocket ship.

I wasn't ready to give up yet.

Finding investors that fit

Three different people in my network recommended I speak to the VC firm Venrex Investment Management, and all of them separately and very kindly made a personal introduction for me.

This was something Venrex couldn't ignore: they invited me in to pitch. I met the partners, Mark and Tom, expecting the usual 30 minutes of airtime and the standard 'Come back when you've got more progress' line – but three hours later, we were still talking. I had our beautiful shoes and packaging out on the table, the discussion flowed, and I had a growing sense that the fit was perfect.

These were smart guys with an incredibly impressive portfolio of start-ups, half of which were run by female founders – unheard of! – with a strong leaning towards e-commerce, fashion and lifestyle. Mark and Tom were normal, likeable, friendly, good-humoured – just really nice guys. I wanted to hang out with them and talk business forever.

Three days later, I was in a local cafe working on my laptop when I got a call from Mark. After a few introductory pleasantries he paused, and I held my breath in anticipation. Then he simply said:

'We are in.'

Three little words that changed the trajectory of my life.

'Julia,' he said, with a big grin on his face that I could feel radiating down the line, 'We want to invest half a million pounds in your business. We believe in you.'

It's hard to describe the feeling when I heard those words. I nearly fell to my knees with relief, and shed a few tears of joy. Finally, somebody really believed in us, and I'd secured the funding needed for Katy and I to take Upper Street to the next level.

We were on our way to realising our dreams.

A second VC, the Aspire Fund from the British Business Bank, established to invest in female founders, came in as a co-investor with £250,000. I'd met them at a pitch event earlier in the year (so that wasn't a complete waste of time after all!), and they had partnered with Venrex on several deals, so another good fit.

We had a couple more meetings with Venrex to go through the details of the deal, and Katy flew over to meet them. The legal paperwork took a while, there was a lot to sort out, but finally on the last working day before Christmas – while we were having our very small team Christmas lunch at a restaurant in town – I got the call to say the money had landed in the bank.

What a great present that was! We ordered a bottle of champagne to celebrate, and felt absolutely on top of the world.

Rallying the crowd

Naively, I thought once we'd raised investment, all our problems would be over – but in reality, we just stepped onto the next rung of challenges.

There was a lot to do: recruiting key team members, starting a big technical project to rebuild our 3D shoe designer, redeveloping our shoe range and securing central London retail premises. Ambitiously, we even bought out our US competitors. It wasn't long before I was going back to Venrex for follow-on investment, which they were happy to put in. Like all experienced VCs, they had expected we might need it.

It was around December 2014, when again we were getting short on cash reserves, that we came across the relatively new concept of crowdfunding. This was a way of raising investment where you put your business and offer to investors up on a website, and hundreds of everyday, as well as professional, investors can put as little as £10 into your fundraising campaign, to own a share of your company.

I loved the idea of giving our customers, fans and everyone else in our network the opportunity to own a piece of Upper Street and play a genuine part in our growing success. I also thought crowdfunding would be a great marketing tool: raising awareness of our brand not only with consumers, but also with the wider investment community.

There were risks in this fundraising strategy, for sure. We would have to share detailed information about the business in the public arena, and if we didn't make our fundraising target, we'd get zero money – plus risk damaging our brand reputation.

Was this the right thing for a luxury fashion brand to do? Still, this pioneering and democratic route to raising investment had great appeal. With the full backing of our investors, we went for it. The team pulled out all the stops, gathering the information that the crowdfunding platform needed on the business, creating a crowdfunding video and planning the marketing activity.

Within just a month, our campaign was live.

To say the crowdfunding experience was a washing machine of emotions is an understatement. It's incredibly exposing, putting your business out there in the public domain, asking people to invest in you. And it's impossible to relax as every day (hour, minute, second) you compulsively and obsessively look at how close (or far away) you are from reaching your target – knowing that if you don't make it, it could mean curtains for the business.

Our campaign started well. We had a big chunk of money pledged towards our crowdfunding target from Venrex, which was critical in giving other potential investors the confidence to invest, and an early rush of our strongest supporters piled in to back us. But then momentum flattened out, and there were several 'tumbleweed' weeks where few pledges were made.

It was a real grind, but we kept on sending out the marketing messages to our email database and on social media. As we entered the final few weeks, urgency to invest before the deadline kicked in, with a flurry of new backers making their commitments. Successfully reaching the finishing line at the end of our 60-day campaign felt like doing the last mile of a marathon – but we made it, and raised well over our target of £200,000.

Now with two major VCs backing us, several key angel investors and a few hundred everyday crowdfunding investors on board, the responsibility I felt in delivering results loomed large. We continued executing on our plans to grow the business, developing a design-your-own bag range, recruiting stylists to run customer shoe design appointments, and ramping up marketing spend. Our in-store operation was going well, and customers adored visiting our 'Shoe Lounge' to try on and design their creations with our team of experts.

But the technical rebuild of our 3D shoe designer was challenging, and delays in its launch slowed our anticipated growth in sales. We needed further investment; it really did feel like fundraising was a constant activity now.

Preparing our second crowdfunding round in September 2015 was straightforward, as we knew what we were doing; but behind the scenes, cash was getting very tight. I had left it very late in the day to raise this time, and the list of suppliers we owed money to was growing by the day. Nonetheless, I had confidence we would make it: as soon as we'd completed this crowdfund all would be fine, wouldn't it?

I pushed our campaign live.

From funding to failure

Just a few short weeks later, it all fell apart. We had been working on the assumption that Venrex would put more funding into this campaign, but it transpired they had reached the limit of how much they could invest in us, according to the rules of the UK Enterprise Investment Scheme (EIS, a government scheme that gives generous tax breaks to early-stage investors), so they couldn't make it work.

Without our lead investor (our first committed major investor), we had no momentum on the campaign. And although the pledges were coming in, it was a genuine struggle to get our total amount of committed funding moving. We got stuck at around 20 per cent of our target, and it didn't look good: until the figure reaches more than 50 per cent, it can be hard to get floating investors to commit.

I didn't have any other lead investors in the wings.

And I had a horrible sinking feeling that this time, we had run out of luck.

I called a board meeting. We all sat round the table: Venrex, Aspire, Katy on video call and me. After discussing the options, we took the tough call to close the business and take it into administration: as directors, we couldn't continue running the business in the red, and investment wasn't forthcoming at the 11th hour.

Katy and I could have bought the business out of administration and rebuilt it from scratch, but neither of us had the appetite to go right back to the beginning after seven long years – if we couldn't make a big dent in the world, what was the point?

My heart was heavy, but I also felt a tremendous sense of relief. It was like taking off a heavy, wet fur coat and being able to breathe again.

The next couple of months were really tough, making staff redundant, breaking the news to our loyal customer base, and informing our crowdfunding investors of the bad news. We had put our heart and soul into Upper Street – and all our own personal resources – the last thing we ever wanted was to have to close the doors, but in the end, lack of funding certainly contributed to our downfall.

With just a couple of wrong steps, our luck had turned on a pinhead.

What did I learn?

With some time for reflection, I took solace in knowing that very few start-ups make it into successful scale-ups – and that failure is part of the game. I go by that adage that if you haven't failed, you haven't tried hard enough.

And to give myself credit, although the story of Upper Street didn't have the ending we had hoped and planned for, we had enjoyed enormous success along our journey, as we strived to build our high-growth venture.

However, I realised there were some fundraising fundamentals I didn't fully understand before I started this journey:

- I didn't foresee we would need so much funding to build a business at scale, so raising investment wasn't even on my agenda.
- I had no clue that raising investment would be such a critical part of my role as CEO, and that I'd need to lead multiple fundraising rounds.
- I didn't understand the investment ecosystem, or what options were available to me.
- I had little insight into what investors were looking for, how to speak their language, or how to overcome gender bias.
- I didn't really understand what getting on board with a VC meant, and assumed they would just keep on following their money.
- I didn't know how dangerous it was to fail to scenario plan, or build in a cash contingency for things going wrong.
- I failed to realise the importance of mapping out our long-term investment needs, and building a strong pipeline of investors to meet them.

A phoenix from the flames

I became convinced there could be huge value in sharing the lessons I had learned in raising investment for my start-up with others going down that same path. I wanted to prevent founders from falling into the fundraising rabbit holes I'd gone down, short cut their success and empower them to build long-term value for themselves, their customers and investors.

I was also extremely concerned about how little investment was going to female founders, and felt compelled to do my part to address this.

Within a month I set up my next venture, Enter The Arena, a coaching and advisory business with a mission to empower female founders to raise investment and onwards to the exponential growth of their business.

I'm proud to say that Enter The Arena is a successful business. Over the last seven years, we've helped more than 1,400 female founders navigate the fundraising path and scale their businesses to new heights.

It's a privilege to work with such incredible women who are trailblazers in their industries, and I learn from and am inspired by them every day.

So if you're building a business to scale, if you think you might need to raise investment – you're in the right place.

2
Battling the gender funding gap

Female founders are a great bet for investors, outperforming our male counterparts when it comes to building, scaling and growing value in our start-ups.

- Women are considered more effective in 84 per cent of the competencies that are measured most frequently in leaders,[1] such as taking initiative, acting with resilience, practising self-development, driving for results and displaying high integrity and honesty.
- Female-led businesses employ 2.5 times more women,[2] have more satisfied employees,[3] lower incidences of financial misconduct[4] and better corporate social responsibility.[5]
- Companies with female founders perform 63 per cent better than those of their male peers in delivering value for their investors.[6]
- Only 23 per cent of female-led businesses fail, opposed to 34 per cent of male-led businesses.[7]
- Female-led businesses generate 10 per cent more revenue, and deliver double (yes, double!) the return on investment.[8]

These statistics tell an incredibly positive story. Hold on to them as encouragement, as we take a closer look at why so little venture funding goes to women, and the impact of this.

Access to funding

Access to funding is the top barrier to entrepreneurship for women across the entire entrepreneurial journey, with female founders feeling 81 per cent less likely than men that they can access the finance they need for their start-up.[9]

Women still aren't getting their share of the money, lead fewer investment deals and raise significantly smaller amounts than our male counterparts.

Although around one-third of businesses are set up by women,[10] not enough of us are building and leading scale-up businesses:

- five times more men than women go on to build scale-up businesses turning over more than £1 million
- only 8 per cent of high-growth companies acquired between 2001 and 2018 had at least one female founder
- only three out of the 19 high-growth companies floated on the London Stock Exchange during this time were founded by women.[11]

What lies behind female founders' concerns that they don't have 'access to funding'? Are women blocked from the world of investment?

The pale, stale and male world of venture capital

The venture funding industry, like many, was established – and continues to be run predominantly – by white men.

Even now, as we push to get more diversity into the world of venture capital, only between 15 and 18 per cent[12] of angel investors are women, and 83 per cent[13] of senior VC investment teams have no women on their investment committees deciding which start-ups to back.

It's a system that, left unchecked, is stacked against women and other under-represented founders, whether it's race, gender, age, social background or disability.

Male VC partners are half as likely as their female counterparts to invest in start-ups with a woman on the senior team, and three times less likely to invest in those with a female CEO.[14]

Investors tend to have a bias towards backing businesses and founders they understand and relate to. They'll source deals from their existing networks; their conscious and unconscious biases lead them to make their mind up about you before you even walk through the door; and when you do get through that door, they ask you very different questions than they ask a man.

They'll think twice or three times about backing you, just because you're a woman.

Gender biases

We're fighting against conditioned subconscious beliefs that people have held for centuries about the traditional female role in society, and how capable women might be at building and scaling businesses.

To illustrate how ingrained these biases can be, a study where VCs were observed as they discussed funding applications and entrepreneurial potential, revealed just how differently they referred to male and female founders (Table 1).

Table 1: How investors describe entrepreneurs by gender[15]

Male entrepreneur attributes	Female entrepreneur attributes
'Young and promising'	'Young, but inexperienced'
'Arrogant, but very impressive competence'	'Lacks network contacts and in need of help to develop her business concept'
'Aggressive, but a really good entrepreneur'	'Enthusiastic, but weak'
'Experienced and knowledgeable'	'Experienced, but worried'
'Very competent innovator and already has money to play with'	'Good-looking and careless with money'
'Cautious, sensible, and level-headed'	'Too cautious and does not dare'
'Extremely capable and very driven'	'Lacks ability for venturing and growth'
'Educated engineer at a prestigious university and has run businesses before'	'Visionary, but with no knowledge of the market'

Source: Table reproduced by kind permission of *Harvard Business Review*. Originally published under the English title 'We recorded VCs' conversations and analyzed how differently they talk about female entrepreneurs', by Malim Malmstrom, Jeaneth Johansson and Joakim Wincent, in the issue May 2017. Copyright © 2017 by Harvard Business Publishing; all rights reserved.

Prevention questions

Research also shows that female founders are more often asked 'prevention questions' that look at potential loss, rather than 'potential questions' that focus on possible gain.[16] It's quite a marked difference, with two-thirds of the questions that women are asked being preventative, versus two-thirds of the questions that men are asked being promotional. For example:

- **Prevention** – 'How will you stop competitors taking your market share?'
- **Promotion** – 'How will you scale to capture market share?'

Being asked these type of questions puts women on the defensive, which then limits how investors perceive their potential.

Pregnancy and children

Female founders often get very different questions in their interactions with investors around their personal and family life. Frequently, assumptions are made that you'll probably have a baby soon – if you haven't already got one – and conclusions are drawn that you might change your focus away from building your start-up, or that you're 'just running a lifestyle business'.

Women are twice as likely to report investor bias when they're pregnant or have children.[17] Of course, the reality is that you may not have children, want them or be able to have them; but if you do, there are many ways of balancing family life with building a high-growth start-up.

It's frustrating that male founders simply don't get asked these questions.

How female founders look and sound

Not only are women dealing with general bias against our gender when raising investment, but it's been shown that how attractive you are as a female founder also comes into play when determining how likely you are to succeed in fundraising.[18]

It may shock you to learn that highly attractive women are statistically *less* likely to secure investment, than women who are deemed less attractive. The opposite applies to male founders: the more attractive they are, the more likely they are to get funding.

Draw your own conclusions on this, but one might infer that male investors find it harder to imagine an attractive woman in any other role than a sexual one, while they see an attractive male as someone who can be way more successful in business (Figure 1).

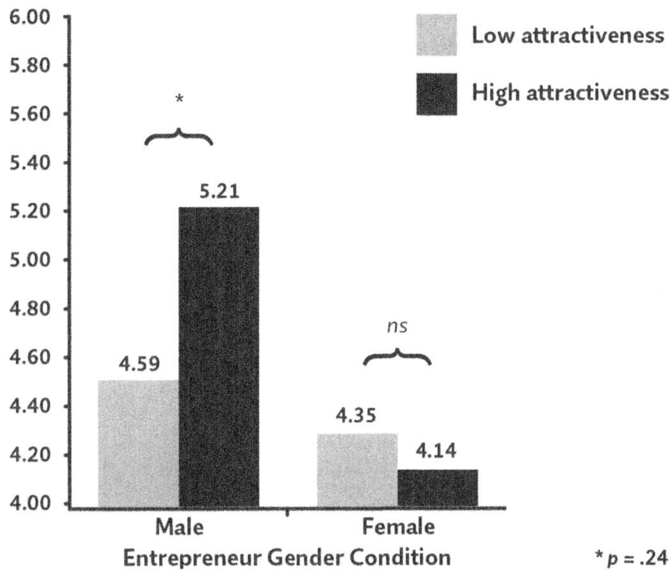

Figure 1: The effect of entrepreneur gender and physical attractiveness on pitch success rate

Source: Alison Wood Brooks, Laura Huang, Sarah Wood Kearney and Fiona E. Murray, Massachusetts Institute of Technology 2014 (*www.pnas.org/content/111/12/4427*). (Reproduced with kind permission of PNAS.)

This research was extended to another study,[19] where identical pitches were presented by male and female voices only, without revealing the founders themselves, and randomly shown to investors. Of the investors, 68 per cent chose to fund ventures pitched by a male voice, while only 32 per cent selected pitches with a female voice.

Venturesplaining

As the evidence shows, female founders are often seen by venture capitalists as less experienced than their male counterparts, even with the same number of years working in an industry.

This unconscious bias can show up directly in the way investors speak to female founders. It's a common complaint among women seeking funding that male investors will patronisingly explain to you how your industry or business works, or how your customers think and feel – when the reality is that you know significantly more about this than they do. They assume you don't understand because you're a woman; they talk at you, don't ask questions, don't listen or show real interest in your opinions.

This insidious (and incredibly annoying) behaviour displayed by many men in the venture industry – especially those who believe themselves to be in a position of power – is encapsulated in a term I have coined: 'venturesplaining'. You'll probably recognise it as a derivation of 'mansplaining', a concept outlined by feminist writer Rebecca Solnit, who wrote an essay on how 'men explain things to me' in 2008.[20]

The dangerous outcome of venturesplaining is that female founders can leave the interaction feeling 'less than', with their skills and experience minimised, confidence chipped and questioning their own expertise. This perpetuates the problem of female founders' lack in confidence and struggle to raise investment.

We'll be looking at how to deal with gender bias throughout this book.

Industry initiatives to redress the gender funding gap

There are numerous reports on the worrying state of female founder investment that examine global and national trends, many of which are referenced throughout this book. For example, in 2019, the UK Government commissioned the Rose Review of Female Entrepreneurship[21] (which I was a contributor to), and as a consequence launched the Investing in Women Code, to improve female founders' access to tools, resources and finance from the financial services sector.[22]

Many large corporates including banks, accounting, legal and technology firms are putting sponsorship money into initiatives to support female founders, promote diversity in VC, and put pressure on the government to look at proper measurement of the gender funding gap and diversity targets.

There are also several entrepreneurial and women-in-business networks that are working hard to level the playing field through events, workshops and community support (more of which you can read about in the Further Resources section at the end of this book).

Despite the ongoing work in the start-up ecosystem to raise awareness of the gender funding gap, encourage more diversity of investors, better measure and track diversity in funding opportunities and outcomes, and provide more comprehensive support for female founders, there is still a very long way to go before we have a level playing field. Stereotypes can be slow to die and systems hard to change, especially when they suit those who both designed and benefit from them.

It's an unfortunate reality that as a female founder in a male-dominated investment world, you may still face either conscious or unconscious bias, and have to work just that little bit harder to get your fundraise done. But we mustn't let the headline data stop us from embarking on raising investment in the first place, otherwise the statistics become a self-fulfilling prophecy.

It's incredible to think that if women set up and scaled businesses at the same rate as men, we would have 1.1 million more businesses, generating £250 billion for the UK economy each year.[23]

However, there are many encouraging signs on the fundraising front. More first-time fundraises are being led by women now, at 22 per cent[24] up from only 5 per cent 10 years ago – meaning that there is a much stronger pipeline of female founders coming through.

In addition, first-time female-founded businesses have similar rates of 'follow-on' funding to the guys (further investment after their first seed funding round), proving that once we've got some backing, we're on our way.[25]

It's time to empower yourself with the strategy, skills and support you need to raise investment.

3
Should you raise investment?

What is investment?

In the context of the start-up world, investment is 'equity finance'. You might also hear this called 'venture finance' or 'venture capital'.

Equity finance is where you sell shares in your company in return for cash. This investment can come from individuals with money, called 'angels' or 'High Net Worth Individuals' (HNWIs). It also can come from organisations that manage money on behalf of others in a fund, such as VC firms, corporate venturing arms or private equity firms. Equity crowdfunding platforms are often used to bring together lots of investors on a deal. (We'll be looking at all these investor types in more detail in Chapter 9.)

Investors put their money into your company now, hoping you'll grow the business over time, sell it for vast amounts of money and at that point, they will get an incredible return on their investment.

VC is a risky investment class: on average, three-quarters of venture-backed start-ups fail,[1] so wise investors factor that in by spreading their portfolio wide. Because of that risk, investors are looking for significant potential returns when you ultimately sell your business for a great deal more than it's worth today.

Does your business need investment?

Securing equity finance isn't the be-all and end-all for a start-up, despite what you may have been led to believe. Many times I've listened to founders tell me their business goal is to raise a 'Series A' (investment round of several million pounds), or read about a founder lauded in the press because of their amazing multimillion-pound fundraise, despite big question marks around whether that business can ever be viable.

Sure, it's validating to know that others want to back you – but fundraising is not a goal. Rather, it's a tool to help you get your business to where you want it to be.

Investment is money: it's resource, fuel.

An injection of money into your business is something you may or may not need. If you're able to scale your company to healthy profitability without taking on external investment, you'll own it 100 per cent, and reap all the benefits in the long term. Indeed, the whole point of having a business is to make it profitable one day, otherwise you'll come undone at some point.

Ask yourself these questions:

- Could I scale the business even further faster, if I had an extra injection of cash?
- Do I have competitors hot on my heels – if I don't grow fast, I'll fall behind and fail?
- Does my business need economies of scale or a critical mass of customers to be viable – I need a volume of business quickly to get to profitability?

- Do I need to make major investments into the business for growth that I can't cover from cash flow? For example, investments in product development, stock, taking on new team members, building technology, physical assets or major marketing campaigns?

Of businesses, 82 per cent fail due to of lack of funding.[2] If you're an ambitious entrepreneur who wants to scale your business and achieve your dreams, the chances are you might need to get your hands on some rocket fuel to help you there.

Is investment right for you?

Three things make a business work for you as a founder:

- **income** – the financial rewards
- **lifestyle** – the freedom to enjoy that money
- **contribution** – feeling good about what you're doing.

This blend of income, lifestyle and contribution can be achieved in two different ways when building and growing a business: one of which isn't a fit for investment, while the other is.

Lifestyle business

A lifestyle business is one that a founder typically sets up to provide the life they want *right now*: a good salary, comfortable work–life balance and doing something they love. This type of business usually has limited ability to scale, and is often found in the creative industries where there is a sole founder or partnership.

A lifestyle business tends to be accessible for many entrepreneurs, as it doesn't need huge capital to launch or sustain.

If you're building a lifestyle business, venture funding isn't a fit for you: investors won't be able to see how their money will grow or how they'll be able to get it back out, given that you're not looking to scale and exit for a multiple valuation.

If you're running a charity, social enterprise or community interest company (i.e. not for private profit), equity funding won't be right for you either, for the same reasons.

High-growth business

If you're building a business you plan to scale into something much bigger, so you can sell it in the future for a significant amount of money, this is a high-growth start-up or value-driven business. The risk here is usually high, because more capital is required to launch and develop the company; however, this is counterbalanced against future rewards, when hopefully you exit the business for a huge valuation.

Building a high-growth start-up often means making sacrifices around short-term income or lifestyle, as revenue is reinvested in the business and the founder works extremely hard to achieve growth.

If you're building this kind of business, equity funding might be a good fit for you: you may well need investment to help you achieve high growth, plus investors will be attracted to the opportunity due to the financial return they could make.

With a high-growth business, it's important to be aware of what taking on investors really means.

Investment means shared ownership

Your new investors become part-owners of your business. How much influence and control they have in the company depends on the deal you strike. Be aware that this partnership is like getting married – except it's harder to get rid of investors you've fallen out of love with than it is to get a divorce!

Be sure to step into that partnership with your eyes wide open.

Investment brings accountability

Once you have investors in your business, you're no longer just accountable to yourself. You must run board meetings and keep investors informed, and have proper discipline, processes and accountability on running the business.

This can be a real period of 'growing up' in in your company, which you may or may not welcome.

Investment drives you to exit

As soon as you have investors on board, you need to be on a path to exit. The goal now is about growing, scaling and selling the company, because that's the only way investors are going to get their returns.

Make sure that this is the way you want to go.

Is your business investable?

If you're comfortable with the concept of taking on investment, the question now turns to how attractive your business might be for investors.

At the most basic level, investors are looking for a return on their money within a reasonable time frame. They want to know that you:

- have a great idea and a great team
- are proving the concept in the market
- have the ability to scale and exit.

Here are five questions to ask yourself:

1. Am I solving a real and pressing problem for my customers?
2. Am I proving this by generating growing amounts of revenue?
3. Can I see how the business can be profitable?
4. Am I doing it better than anyone else in the market?
5. Is there a vast market out there for me to capture?

If you can answer 'Yes' to all of those, your business *could* be a good fit for equity finance – although the stage your business is at can be a factor too.

Funding stages

It's worth understanding at this point the types of funding as they are known in the start-up industry, as you'll hear these terms referred to frequently: pre-seed, seed, 'Series A' and 'Series B'.

Pre-seed

This is investment secured prior to business launch, used to develop the concept and get operations off the ground. It's usually funded by the founders, perhaps also along with friends and family.

Seed

This is the first 'official' funding to enable the business to finance its early years, from launch through to initial traction (i.e. progress in the market). It's usually provided by professional investors, often also by the founders and their close contacts, with investment amounts ranging from the low tens of thousands to a few million pounds.

Series A+

Later funding rounds are called 'Series A', 'Series B' and so on. These kick in once your business is more established, with funding amounts of £2–3 million or more to support business growth at scale.

When's the right time to raise?

Ask most entrepreneurs when they want to raise investment by, and they'll tell you they need the money yesterday! However, there are some sweet spots when raising investment is going to be easier for you.

When you're pre-launch

It can be tough to raise investment from professional investors when you're right at the beginning of your venture with just a concept or a business plan. It's high-risk: most investors will tell you to come back and see them when you're further along. There are a few caveats to this.

First, if you're a successful serial entrepreneur (i.e. you've had one or two businesses already that you've launched, scaled and sold), investors may be prepared to back you on an idea only. They have more faith that you'll make a success of things, as you've done it before.

Second, if you have an incredibly compelling idea in an incredibly compelling market, you *might* raise money from professional investors right at the start – but this is very rare.

When you have traction

Securing equity investment is much easier at a point when you have traction in your business. There is no precise definition of what traction equates to, but fundamentally it's showing proof that your business is growing, and that its growth rate is accelerating: evidencing that the market wants what you've got, and your business has potential.

The more you can demonstrate that you have paying customers, great customer feedback, returning clients, etc. and that your business is operationally effective, the better. These things help show an investor that you might deliver a good return on their investment, if they back you.

When you've just completed a key milestone that proves traction, you have a powerful story to tell investors – this is a superb time to raise money.

When you still have money in the bank

Don't leave raising investment to the point when you're out of cash, as you're in a much weaker position at the point of desperation.

If possible, make sure you have a good six-months' worth of money in the bank when you go out to raise. If you know what you're doing, a well-run fundraising campaign can take around four to six months from start to finish, sometimes a little longer.

Also, bear in mind that certain periods in the year can impact the timescales on raising money, as the investment industry tends to go a little quiet in the school holidays. Meanwhile, the weeks towards the end of the accounting financial year are also busy times for investors, so be sure to plan accordingly.

Raise money when you've got some proof points, but before you need it.

STORY: A SOUND POSITION TO RAISE

May Al-Karooni, Globechain

Globechain is the leading environmental social governance data reuse marketplace that connects enterprises with non-profits, small businesses and people to redistribute unneeded items. Founder and CEO May Al-Karooni bootstrapped the business for four years, winning contracts with world-leading brands and mentorship from retail giant eBay, before turning to fundraising to fuel her company's growth.

For May, it was all about timing.

> *'I wasn't expecting Globechain to be big at first – I just had an idea, and wanted to see if it would work. I was initially against going for fundraising; I didn't feel like I needed it straight away. It wasn't on my mind to do this whole "tech start-up" thing.*
>
> *But by year four the business was really growing, and it was ridiculous; I was working 24 hours a day. We could have plodded on nice and steadily for years, but that's not how start-up models work. You've got to be first-to-market, you've got to watch your back for competition.*
>
> *So I thought deeply about my vision, and what I wanted the business to be. I decided I wanted this to be a huge business – to make it global.*
>
> *After four years I was in a sound position to raise because the company was generating revenue, and I could prove it.'*

Other sources of money

Equity finance isn't the only way to plug your funding gap. There are lots of other options to consider, if:

- your business is still at idea or pre-launch stage
- you don't need tens of thousands of pounds
- you need some bridging money to tide you over
- you're not planning to scale to exit.

Bootstrapping

At the start of your business growth journey, consider using any savings you might have, or use credit cards (ideally on a 0 per cent interest deal), which can be a great way to get out of the blocks quickly.

Focus on generating revenue, and reinvest your profits. Many founders also stay in full or part-time employment during this phase to provide an income and, where possible, invest any disposable income into the business.

Rewards-based crowdfunding

This type of crowdfunding can be a great way to launch a new product, by creating a sales page on the crowdfunding platform, and allowing customers to pre-purchase your product before you've developed and produced it. This raises the funds you need in advance, while also validating the market.

However, you'll probably need to invest at least some money in marketing your campaign – so do be prepared for that.

Loans

Securing a business loan can be a great option for early-stage businesses. Your business bank is a great place to start; also, do check what loan schemes might be available locally to you.

For example, at the time of writing, in the UK there is the government-backed Start-up Loan Scheme, where you can get up to £25,000 on a personal loan basis.

Don't forget, you may need to underwrite any loan you take out, or secure it against assets such as any property you might own. It's important you feel comfortable with taking on that risk, and can plan how you will pay back both the interest on the loan and the loan capital itself (often, loans are also referred to as 'debt').

Grants

A grant is a sum of money given to a start-up to develop the business, which can come from national or local government initiatives, charity or industry. Often the money is provided retrospectively after you've spent it, and tied to a specific project you're undertaking: that is, making advancements in a particular area, for example technology, science or social development.

Grant applications are notoriously complex, so you may need support with this.

Research and development tax credits

If your business requires research and development (R&D) investment, you might qualify for government tax relief on the amount of money spent on these initiatives. Your accountant or R&D tax specialist firm can support you with your application, if you need it.

Invoice financing

If your business trades with customers on lengthy payment terms, you can look to secure invoice financing. You receive the money ahead of time on credit and get the cash now, in exchange for a fee charged by the invoice financing company (typically 2–3 per cent of the value of the invoice), instead of waiting for that invoice payment 30, 60 or 90 days down the line. This is also sometimes referred to as 'factoring'.

Marketing financing

If you're an e-commerce business with proven online advertising funnels, generating more than £10,000 in monthly recurring revenue, you may be able to secure advanced funding based on your future e-commerce sales.

Providers take a percentage of your revenue each month for the loan repayment plus their fees, often on flexible terms – but you do need to be reasonably established to qualify.

(See the Further Resources at the end of this book, where you'll find some useful contacts for these alternative funding resources.)

If you've explored and/or exhausted these options, are sure you need to raise a decent chunk of money, understand the implications of taking on investment and have got at least some early proof points in your business, then raising investment is where you might head next.

Are you ready for the ride?

4
Fundraising mindset

As you prepare for raising investment, you might feel terrified at this point, with a voice deep down inside telling yourself that you're not good enough: that your business isn't good enough, and worrying that investors won't want to talk to 'little old me'. You just might not feel in a positive place right now.

Conversely, you might be feeling full of optimism and positivity – but as you hit bumps along the fundraising road, there will be times when that confidence can get knocked. The extra factor that makes the difference between failure and success on your journey, providing you with bulletproof confidence, is a fundraising mindset.

As such, this is probably the most important chapter in this book, and a great place to come back to any time you need a mindset top-up.

Your inner world reflects outwards

Your business is just like a mirror: it reflects all the things going on in your mind. All your fears and beliefs, everything you think you're good or terrible at, and your insecurities. When we think something isn't working, the mistake we often make as founders is trying to change the business. We fiddle around with our financial forecast, marketing strategy, product or website – and this is just as crazy as looking in the mirror, not liking our reflection, then taking out a big black pen and drawing on the glass!

A great example of this is the TV show, *The Hotel Inspector*. When you see the scion of the Forte hotel dynasty and businesswoman, Alex Polizzi, troubleshooting a failing hotel business, you realise that the problem is rarely in the actual business; it's almost always in the business owner, who has fears or insecurities. Ninety per cent of the work Alex does is in their mindset: once that's right, everything else flows from there.

Even if you have a few people working for you, you are your business, so it's about fixing what's going on between your ears – which can be scary, as it means the responsibility lies with you.

The good news is that it's so much easier to change yourself, than if there were something wrong with your business.

Limiting beliefs

Limitations that others place on us – that we consequently place on ourselves – can start almost as soon as we're born, and continue through our formative years and beyond. Gender role expectations in society, lack of role models and educational experience can condition girls into thinking of roles and careers revolving around societal stereotypes of nurturing and appearance – which can influence our beliefs about what's possible for us in business.

Girls as young as seven feel they can't say or do what they want, and this can influence how much they take part in school,[1] resulting in only a quarter[2] of girls taking science, technology, engineering and maths (STEM) subjects at secondary or high school. As such, it's not surprising that women occupy just 17 per cent of technology jobs, 4 per cent of software engineer roles, make up only 3 per cent of VC partners, and a tiny 1 per cent of leadership positions within STEM-focused sectors.[3]

Moreover, only one-third of women feel they have the skills, knowledge and experience they need to start a business, compared with half of men. And only 62 per cent of women have some understanding of how they might fund their business, versus 79 per cent of men.[4]

Acknowledge any limiting beliefs you might hold and recognise them for what they are: *they are just beliefs*, which doesn't make them true. It's never too late to upskill, especially when it comes to learning how to raise investment.

It's possible to achieve anything you want, when you put your mind to it.

STORY: FINDING YOUR COURAGE

Savannah de Savary, Built-ID

Built-ID is a property technology (PropTech) company which enables collaboration through innovative technology, empowering communities to have a meaningful impact on property development in their neighbourhood.

Savannah started the business after working in the real estate development industry for two years. She was just 23 years old when she took the plunge and gave up her employed role. She initially raised around £1.7 million through angel investors and a specialist PropTech VC to get her start-up off the ground, before a further equity raise of £2 million to support growth.

Asking for investment didn't come easily to Savannah, but getting the right support was a real turning point for her.

'I hated asking for things, so fundraising felt like my worst nightmare. I went to so many fundraising meetings where I've not had the courage to say, "Are you interested in investing?" and instead I just said, "Thank you so much for your advice, good day!" Asking for things doesn't come naturally to me, but you can't get anywhere without it.

The real turning point for me was to get a professional coach, which I wish I'd invested in far earlier than I did. It's expensive, but it's worth every penny. It's not like they tell you the answers; they just help you figure out what you already probably knew deep down, delving into questions like:

Why do you hate asking people for money?

Why do you hate asking people for help, full stop?

What's the worst that can happen if they say "No"?

Is it not worse than feeling like a failure because you never picked up the courage to ask?

I couldn't recommend enough having people to help coach you in those tough times and the good times.'

Build confidence

We hear a lot about women having less confidence than men, and that's what holds us back – but is it true? We know women are rated as great leaders, but when we're asked to self-assess on competencies, we give ourselves way less generous ratings,[5] and evidence suggests that women tend to feel less comfortable about putting their ambitions out there.[6]

The good news is that over time, our confidence increases. From a career perspective, by the time we get to mid-life, our confidence levels are on a par with men – and by the time we sail past 60, our confidence also surpasses them. With the average age of a high-growth potential founder being 45,[7] this bodes well for women.

It's important to remember that most founders are doing things every day that they've never done before, and this continual path of learning and being out of our comfort zone is half the fun of the entrepreneurial journey.

Raising investment will almost certainly take you outside your comfort zone, and the chances are you're going to encounter some obstacles along the way. If you have the guts to go out there to get what you want, and the tenacity to keep going until you get there, nothing can stop you from raising the investment you need.

Your confidence will come from learning the skills of fundraising and putting them into practice.

STORY: STRENGTH OF CONVICTION

Sophie Hooper, Secret Saviours

Sophie Hooper was the Managing Director of Team Saatchi, a division of Saatchi & Saatchi UK, working with high-profile beauty and healthcare brands, when she met the inventor of new clinically-proven stretch mark prevention technology, and spotted the commercial opportunity for the concept.

She left her successful corporate career to run the company, putting in all her savings (plus those of her family and friends) to develop the product into something women would love to wear, to create and build the Secret Saviours brand and take the product to market.

To date, Sophie has raised more than £2 million in equity finance, and saved more than 17,000 women from stretch marks.

Her confidence in her product is one of the key things that drives her on fundraising:

'I can't say it's been an easy ride, throwing a salary in like that and entering the unknown. But I absolutely knew it was going to work. I still sit here now and absolutely know that.

Yes, it was a risk, but I had the strength of conviction to know that there's a need for our product, and it solves a previously unsolvable problem. It has to work, because this is it for me! I've put everything into this business, and it's not going to fail. It's what gets me out of bed every morning and keeps me going. The product is too good not to, and it's my duty to get it out there.

Investors buy into the person, and they've got to see belief. Investors can either see desperation or determination. They want to know that you're not going to let this fail. They tell me that my passion, drive and commitment are what they are drawn to.

I used to dread investor meetings: you can't help your mind starting to wander off into, "What will you do if you don't get this money?" But I just keep turning back and say to myself: "You're going to, you're going to." I've turned myself around into thinking, "Come on, people are lucky to be involved in this business. This is going to be massive!"

Now I'm not in that panicked mode, and I get investors to pitch to me.

And I'm actually enjoying it.'

Overcome fear of failure

Fear of failure is a key limiting factor for 46 per cent[8] of female founders, and women are less likely to seek finance than their male counterparts because they're worried they won't be successful.[9] However, learning from our mistakes is part of the entrepreneurial process, as we strive to disrupt established ways of doing things. Your journey will undoubtably include many failures – some large, some small.

When it comes to raising investment, two fears can pull a founder in very different directions:

- going out to raise investment and failing
- not raising investment and the business failing.

This push-me-pull-you dilemma can lead to debilitating inertia, as the founder deliberates over whether to raise investment for months, if not years; meanwhile, the business collapses around them.

If the worst possible outcome either way is that you fail to raise investment and your business stagnates or dies, it can be helpful to accept that this may well happen. Coming to terms with that enables you to deal with that fear, and move on to focusing on how to give yourself the best chance of success now.

Another fear that creeps into the minds of many female founders is worry about taking on the wrong investors, and losing control of their business. Once you get a better understanding of how to attract the *right* investors, make sure they're a good fit and negotiate a deal that builds real value for you, you won't feel that fear anymore. Neither will you have to settle for working with the wrong investors.

STORY: A LEAP OF FAITH

Francesca Hodgson, GoodBox

GoodBox helps non-profit organisations take cashless donations by providing them with contactless charity donation boxes, along with software to help them track, analyse and grow the amount of money they raise.

As co-founder of the business, Francesca secured angel investment at idea and proof-of-concept stage and later crowdfunded two rounds, raising in total almost £6 million in investment finance in the first four years of their business. To date, GoodBox has processed more than £5.5 million in cashless donations for more than 1,500 incredible charities across the UK, including the Teenage Cancer Trust, Natural History Museum and Costa Foundation.

Fran's philosophy is that you'll never know success unless you go for it:

> *'I never woke up one day intending to be an entrepreneur. For me, it was a journey I went on throughout my life – looking at what was important to me from a lifestyle point of view, and taking hold of the opportunities that presented themselves. It was about meeting people at the right time, having passion and doing what you love.*
>
> *As an entrepreneur I get to manage my diary, I get to take my kids to school, which for me is invaluable. I enhance my understanding of the world, I get to invest in myself. Ten people can have the same idea, but the reality is in the idea's execution, and being in the right place at the right time with the right people around you.*

My advice when it comes to raising investment is to go for it! Until you take that leap of faith, you'll never know. And remember, it's OK to fail.

As women particularly, we do come down hard on ourselves if we trip and fall at the first hurdle, but we've got to get back up again – and it's only sometimes through those failures that we learn to do it right the next time.'

Prioritise your well-being

Ask any entrepreneur, and they'll tell you they have way too much on their plate. Our modern-day addiction to 'busyness' can be destructive, as we fill our days with endless tasks and to-do lists.

Women still spend a disproportionate amount of time on household chores than men,[10] and almost half of female founders feel their primary care responsibilities are the number one barrier to success in business – which is ironic, given that flexibility in family care is the number one reason that women start a business in the first place.[11]

Whatever your personal circumstances, whether you're a parent or have other major responsibilities outside of running your business, it's important to have strategies in place to help you manage potential overwhelm in life. Building a good support network around yourself, and making space to look after your own well-being, are both key. Leading a start-up doesn't mean you have to put in a 100-hour week – it's about working smarter, not harder. And that principle also applies to the process of raising investment.

Everybody needs time to rest and relax. If you don't properly take care of your mind and body, eventually you'll burn out. Never is self-care so vital as when you're fundraising.

You need to be on the top of your game when speaking with investors: rolling into a meeting with just two hours' sleep, grey and pasty skin through malnutrition and a body that's all seized up, is not the best place to be.

Whatever works for you, schedule some 'me-time' into your diary, and don't let it be moved: exercise, mindfulness, creative pursuits, socialising, having fun or just binge watching your favourite box set on TV. That way, when you go out for investment, you'll be full of energy and ready to perform at your very best.

STORY: FILL YOUR BUCKET

Lina Chan, My Parla

My Parla is a digital health platform that empowers women throughout their fertility journey with easy access to fertility education, specialists, tests, health and wellness tools and a supportive community of women.

It was after founder Lina experienced pregnancy loss and difficulty conceiving that she realised the need for better support for women during this tough time. In 2018, she raised £250,000 in pre-seed funding to get My Parla off the ground, which she secured from institutional investors and angels. In 2020 she was able to raise an additional £250,000 bridge round of interim funding and secure government grant funding.

Lina has simple strategies on how to manage overwhelm:

'How do I manage to run the business, raise investment and have a life? Coffee is number one on my list! I need it every morning. But really, the biggest thing for me is being OK that if I set certain expectations and I don't meet them, I don't badger myself for it. Accepting that things might take a little longer than expected. Being kind with myself when I don't meet those things is important.

It's important to build a really strong team around you, so if you need to step away for a few days or if you can't make those meetings, things don't just collapse. You must be realistic that you can't completely have it all – something will end up giving.

I worked it out with my husband. He asked me, "What is it you need on a daily basis to fill your bucket?" For me, it's movement: it can be 30 minutes at the gym, or an hour's walk. I try to fit it in during 'walking meetings': I invite people to walk with me, or do conference calls as I walk around the block. It's a way for me to get some fresh air, exercise and feel a little stronger. If I don't manage to get an hour in, I'll palm off all three kids to him and I'll run to the gym for a short workout.

Find what is it that energises you and tap into that, because otherwise if you burn out, who benefits from that? Nobody. And find a coach: somebody who's not involved in your business so there are no biases, so they're there for you, so you can be completely vulnerable with them. You need that outlet.

Women are good at showing vulnerability and asking for help. It's what's helped me be able to juggle everything.'

Keep a positive mindset

Fundraising is something you may end up doing time and again as you build and grow your start-up: it's a key part of your role as a founder and entrepreneurial leader. It's important to recognise and accept this early in the journey and embrace it in a positive way, rather than seeing it as a burden that will drag you down.

Use positive thinking to reduce any stress or anxiety you may feel around raising investment. Your subconscious is like a dog: it's the animal part of your brain, and you can train it to help you stay confident and motivated through repetition. Over time and with consistent training, these qualities become part of you and happen on autopilot.

Approach raising investment from the mindset of inevitable success, and you'll project yourself and your business in the most positive way: radiating a confidence that's incredibly attractive for investors.

Mindset techniques

Here are four helpful techniques that will shift your mindset and approach to fundraising and get your confidence sky high, which you may wish to come back to time and time again throughout your fundraising campaign.

Focus on your success, and it will come to you

Close your eyes and imagine that you've already raised investment. Play a movie in your head that shows you the result you want, so you see your business and life as you want it to be.

This gets you into a state of positivity and enthusiasm, rather than fear. It allows your subconscious to kick in and make this success a reality.

Know what you want, and don't settle

Take this vision of your success, and live in the reality of what you visualise with the actions you take every day. You deserve the best, and sometimes that means making hard choices, letting go of things and passing up on opportunities you know aren't right for you.

If you settle, the risk is that you undervalue your business, complete a fundraising deal that's not in your best interest, or end up with investors who want to take you in the wrong direction.

Trust that everything's going to be all right, and believe that the perfect investor is just around the corner.

Visualise and meditate every day

Cultivate focusing on success as part of your daily routine. Imagine what life looks like when you've raised investment and see and feel that right now, in every little detail: make it real.

You might do that visualisation when, for example, you're in the shower, walking the dog or sitting quietly for 20 minutes.

Getting into this mindset at the start of every day stops you spiralling into negativity when you hit challenges on the fundraising journey, and keeps your confidence up.

Prioritise fundraising every day

Raising investment is going to shift the trajectory of your business, and might even be the difference between its success or failure. This work needs to take priority and be right at the top of your to do list – even if it's the biggest, scariest thing on it and you would rather put it off.

STORY: PUTTING THE FUN INTO FUNDRAISING

Sarah Henley, NextUp Comedy

Sarah, the Founder and COO of NextUp Comedy, started a comedy video subscription business with her three male co-founders in 2017 to fill a clear gap in the video-on-demand industry. Sarah's vision is to build NextUp into the worldwide home of live comedy, using her passion for diversity and equality in the arts to make a mark in her industry.

In 2019, NextUp raised £760,000 in investment finance from a mix of angel investors, VC and crowdfunding. Crowdfunding made perfect sense as a strategy for Sarah, as it meant that comedy performers and an enthusiastic audience fan base could all chip in and take a stake in the company's success.

Sarah's light-hearted approach to fundraising makes it less of a burden for her:

> *'The fundraising work is never done – it's just going to be part of your life. It's a bit like parenting: it's not a job you can tick off your list, it keeps going and it doesn't really stop. If you can come to terms with the fact that fundraising is part of your job, it will feel less like a continual burden, or something that's getting in your way.*
>
> *I had to pitch quite a bit, it took up a lot of my time – but it's time well spent because you need investment, and you need those people behind you. It can be frustrating though because you want to be working on the business. it's a balancing act.*
>
> *As a business we have an "all in it together" attitude, celebrating wins and commiserating losses, and the team rallied us through.*

And one of our company values is a sense of light-hearted perspective – we're running a comedy company – we know we're doing something really good and it's important to us, but nobody's dying!'

Introducing the 5 Steps to Fundraising

Kick any limiting beliefs and fears you have right out the window, and build your confidence by educating and empowering yourself with the knowledge of what it takes to succeed in fundraising as a female founder.

Raising investment successfully while running your business, dealing with life and staying sane is about breaking down the task ahead into bite-sized chunks, so you don't become overwhelmed.

There are five key steps to follow (Figure 2).

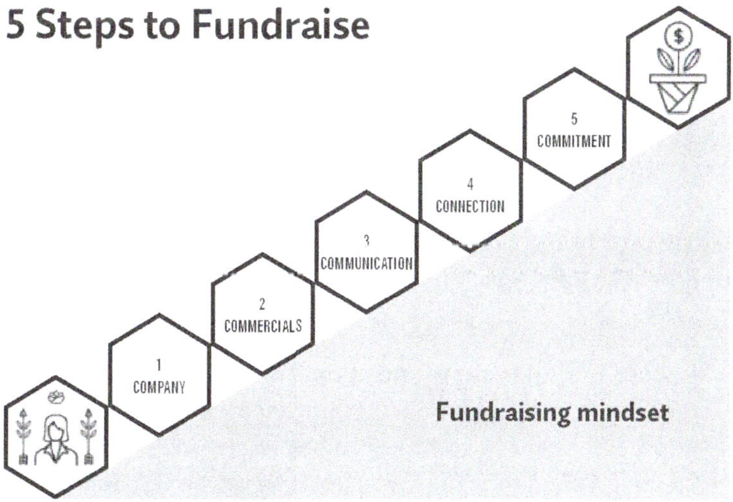

Figure 2: 5 Steps to fundraise

1. **Company** – show you've got an investable business with huge potential to scale, a strong plan for growth and a team that can execute.
2. **Commercials** – demonstrate well thought-through financial projections and an attractive investment deal.
3. **Communication** – explain the opportunity in the language of investors, with a compelling narrative.
4. **Connection** – attract the right investors who will add real value to your business.
5. **Commitment** – run effective investor meetings, and negotiate and close a great deal.

Your fundraising mindset underpins all these steps, as you need to keep that strong throughout the whole fundraising journey.

Why must you get all five right – and in the right order?

- There is no point in spending all your energy connecting with investors, trying to see if they'll back you, if you aren't able to show them you've got a business that's investable or you don't have a sensible deal proposal. The value proposition won't be clear.
- You can have an incredible business, with strong and well-based financial projections, but if you're unable to communicate effectively to potential investors, you're going to get nowhere. They won't be able to see the opportunity.
- Communicating your proposition with well-crafted outreach messages and a stellar investor presentation is all well and good, but if you're speaking to the wrong investors, you're wasting your time. You'll be knocking on closed doors.

- You can do a brilliant job at getting in front of the perfect investor, but if you walk into that meeting and don't know how to handle yourself, can't communicate the opportunity or don't have a clue how to get the best deal, you'll struggle. You won't get an offer, or you'll sign a poor deal that won't benefit you in the long term.

Let's enter the fundraising arena, and take those steps together!

5
Step 1: Company

Every investor has different goals, priorities and ways of looking at whether your company is the right investment opportunity for them. Your first step in the fundraising process is to understand, capture and strengthen in an investment proposal each of the critical areas of your business that investors will be assessing.

This proposal is like a short-form business plan you create for yourself in a simple word processing document, and best written in simple bullet points. It's not a document you'll share with investors, but foundation work to make sure you have covered everything they will want to know.

Before we dive into the details of your investment proposal, let's explore the guiding principles of venture investment.

What outcomes are investors looking for?

Investors are looking to achieve a return on their investment within a reasonable time frame. Investor return requirements vary, but a good rule of thumb is 10 times the money they put in, over a 7–10-year period.

For example, if they invest £100,000 in your company today, in 10 years they would like that to be worth £1 million.

Why do investors want such high returns?

When investors look at your business, they're assessing the risk of your ability to turn the money they commit into more money for them in the future: it's a risk–reward decision. Backing start-ups is a risky business, which is why it's called 'venture'. Investors only make money when their shares in the business are sold for more than they bought them for, when the business is listed on a stock exchange, or the company itself is sold – this is called an 'exit' event.

Recent data show that only 40 per cent of high-growth potential ventures which have raised equity finance go on to scale and exit within eight years; the other 60 per cent have either failed, are stagnating or have yet to exit[1] – and when that happens, the investor's money is either lost or tied up within the business.

Because investors' risk of losing their money is high, the potential returns need to look exciting to counterbalance that risk, otherwise they would be better off putting their money into other, 'safer' investment vehicles such as the stock market, bonds or property.

What else do investors care about?

Financial rewards are important, of course – but like all of us, investors think with their hearts as well as their heads. They want to back a business that resonates with them: something they believe in or feel connected to, that makes a difference in the world.

Plus they want to invest in a company where they feel the fit is right in terms of the demands it will place on them personally, as the business grows:

- the involvement they'll have
- the stress it will cause them
- the enjoyment they'll get out of it
- the value they can add.

Their relationship with you, the founder, is key: they want to work with an entrepreneur they like and respect. In fact, the decision they make to invest is like the one you made when you started your business, and the decision you make every day as you carry on building it:

- It is worth it?
- Can I make money with this venture?
- Will this fit with how I want my life to be?
- Will this make me feel good? (Income – Lifestyle – Contribution.)

How do investors assess the opportunity?

Let's look at the key areas of your investment proposal they really care about, and how you can capture the information they're looking for – note how important it is to have clarity, be thorough in your preparation, and find evidence and data to support your plan. This approach speaks to the rational decision-making process for an investor, raises your gravitas as a female founder, and gives you bulletproof confidence in your proposition.

Vision

How are you making a real difference in the world?

Your vision statement helps investors understand quickly what your business is, your long-term ambition and intended impact. It needs to:

- be expressed simply
- use clear and compelling language
- be ambitious.

(Note that this is not the same as your customer tagline, which is a marketing tool focused on communicating what you provide to customers right now.)

It can be challenging to articulate your vision simply, so you may need to come back to this a few times before you land on something that really works. (See Further Resources for some online resources to help you craft it.)

Problem

What's the problem you're solving in the market?

The more painful this problem is, the more likely your customers will want to find a solution. Get clear on the following:

- *What* is the problem is for your customers?
- *Why* is it such a big deal for them?
- What's the *pain factor?*

Without understanding this, it's difficult to see why the market needs a solution, and so why your business would be investable.

Here's a simple example to illustrate the point: the problems and pain factor that drive demand for a food box subscription service:

- **Problem** – many busy, affluent people who love cooking don't have the time and energy to plan healthy meals for the week, look up all the recipes, build an online shopping list for all the ingredients, then try to get an online delivery slot when they're available or go to the supermarket.
- **Pain factor** – these people either end up with an empty fridge or lots of fresh ingredients that get thrown away, and a lot of time wasted and stress. There is a real emotional and financial impact.

Find evidence to validate that your customers are experiencing this problem, for example through:

- market reports
- your own commissioned research
- quotes from leading industry experts.

This helps to convince investors that this is a problem that really needs solving, rather than expecting them to rely on your intuition as a founder.

Opportunity

What's the size of the opportunity?

Unless a lot of people are looking for a solution to the problem you've identified and it's a growing opportunity, this isn't likely to be a business you can scale and generate a return on investment.

Demonstrate the size of the opportunity with:

- relevant data on the market you're operating in
- customers you're targeting through industry or market reports

- tangible data on the number of customers and value of products in the market.

You may need to make some assumptions about how this data translates into market size. Consider both the market you want to address in the short term (national, regional or perhaps a specific customer segment or part of the market), as well as the long term (which may be global, or address a larger market segment) – and size up the part of the market that is most relevant to you, not just the overall industry value.

Typically, these are the terms investors use when assessing the size of the market opportunity:

- **Total Addressable Market (TAM)** – the total size of the market in which you operate.
- **Serviceable Addressable Market (SAM)** – the size of the market that is relevant to your product or service and is likely to buy.
- **Serviceable Obtainable Market (SOM)** – the size of the market you think it's *likely* you can capture, i.e. market share (Figure 3).

Calculating the size of each of these markets and segments shows investors that you have a realistic sense of the potential revenue your business could generate.

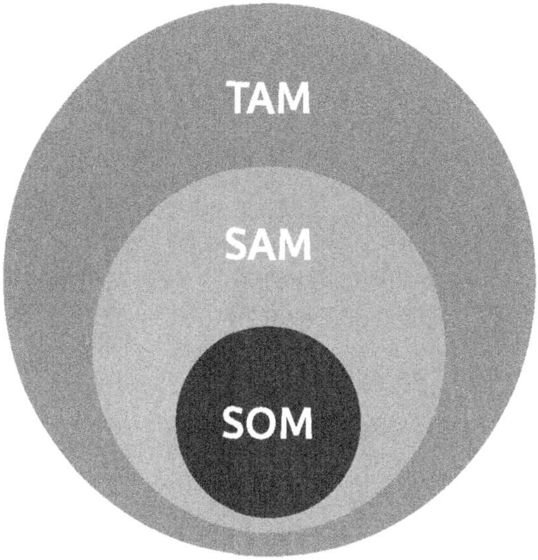

Figure 3: Market opportunity definitions

STORY: HOW BIG COULD THIS GROW?

Nicola Gammon, Shoot

Nicola is the Founder and CEO of Shoot, which operates in the gardening market, selling its online garden design tool and plant reference database to both garden designers and hobby gardeners.

Shoot now has more than 30,000 plants in its database, more than 150,000 members in 87 countries, and has developed software specifically for the needs of garden designers. The more gardens and plants members save in Shoot, the more committed they become to using the service, and the more difficult it is for competitors to enter the marketplace.

Nicola raised £600,000 in equity finance through two crowdfunding rounds and has more than 600 investors on board.

'For me to see the potential to scale Shoot, I wanted to understand the impact of the problem my customers were experiencing, and how many of them might have that problem. I needed to look at two types of customers: those who have their own gardens and do this as a hobby, and professional garden designers who work with people with gardens.

The problem they both experience is quite different, and the size of those two segments is also very different. But I charge different prices to those segments because of the difference in value that Shoot provides. I knew investors would need convincing of the numbers, particularly if they weren't gardeners themselves.

It was pretty easy to find out most of the data I needed, just by searching online and by speaking directly to the organisations and industry bodies in my market. I discovered that the cost of plants being killed is £168 million per year, 50 per cent of gardeners have killed a plant, 90 per cent of plants die because of being planted in the wrong place, and garden designers waste 35 per cent of their time researching plants and creating maintenance guides for clients.

These were compelling statistics that proved what I already knew: that people struggle with plants! And that the current solutions in the market provided online, in books or by garden retailers, were substandard.

Then I learned that the size of the global gardening market is $200 billion [£165 billion], UK spend on gardening is £12.6 billion with year-on-year growth, and in the UK, there are 24 million properties with gardens, 10,000 garden designers and 15 million hobby gardeners.

To work out my market opportunity, I multiplied the number of potential customers by the annual licence or subscription fee I charge.

So, 10,000 UK garden designers @ £390 = £3.9 million, and 15 million hobby gardeners @ £59 = £885 million.

If I could capture 20 per cent of the garden designer market (£3.9 million x 20% = £780,000) and 5 per cent of the hobby gardener market (£885 million x 1% = £8.85 million), I'd be generating around £9.63 million revenue a year.

Armed with all this data, not only did I feel convinced this was a business worth scaling, even if I just looked at the UK market, but I felt confident investors would see the opportunity too.'

Market landscape

What's going on in your market that makes *right now* the ideal time for your start-up to flourish?

It might be because of changes in society, technology, politics, environment or in the competitive environment itself.

Are you riding a wave of change that can propel you even faster into the future? If so, that can make your business even more investable, as people love to back businesses in markets that are on the ascendancy.

Look for market research or industry reports that evidence this.

STORY: A QUESTION OF POWER

Sarah Merrick, Ripple Energy

In 2017, Sarah Merrick was poised to launch the UK's first consumer-owned wind farm, making clean energy ownership affordable and accessible for everyone, everywhere. Although highly experienced in her field, with 16 years of senior management roles in the renewable energy industry, it was Sarah's first time building a start-up and raising investment.

After securing initial pre-seed angel funding of £150,000 in 2018 to get the project off the ground, Sarah secured £856,000 investment the following year through crowdfunding from more than 1,000 investors. Ripple won the award of Start-up of the Year by Seedrs investors and Business Green, and her company continues to thrive.

> *'We funded through friends and family at the start, which was pretty straightforward; it wasn't a hard sell at all. People wanted to get involved and be part of something that was so new. That funding got us to the end of the year, and although we were still pre-launch, we had a couple of hundred customers pre-registered to sign up for Ripple, so we felt that crowdfunding would be the best way of securing further investment.*
>
> *Crowdfunding investors saw the opportunity through their consumer eyes. Their main driver was acting on climate change, which fit with their values, with a second order priority of saving money on their energy bill. It really chimed with them that this was something they'd want to do.*
>
> *In the end, we had 1,080 investors with that campaign, the vast majority of whom we didn't know, and we were in the top 5 per cent of deals by investor numbers on the crowdfunding platform that year – it was just phenomenal.*

We clearly struck a chord: we were right at the start of that changing gear of how individuals viewed climate change.'

Solution

How does your solution address the problem you've identified, and what are the clear benefits for your customers?

Some of the most investable businesses seem to have the most obvious solution, the kind that makes people think: 'Why hasn't someone done that before?'

- Outline your solution in simple terms.
- Map it back to how it solves the problem you've identified.
- Explain the value it provides to your customers.

STORY: FACILITATING BETTER DIVORCES

Pip Wilson, Amicable

Amicable is a lawyer-free alternative to divorce, separation and co-parenting, changing the way people separate for the better. CEO Pip Wilson is an angel investor herself, so had insider knowledge of how investors operate and what they look for.

Pip brought her background in marketing and technology to the table, while her co-founder, Kate, brought knowledge of psychology and family consulting, a blend of skills that are a perfect match for scaling this market-changing business.

To date, Pip has raised a total of £3 million in funding to grow the business over four separate investment rounds.

'My co-founder Kate had her own train wreck of a divorce, which resulted in them spending a lot of money, and going through a huge amount of pain through the whole emotional journey and the courts.

She came out the other side, and said:

"Hold on a minute. It wasn't us that got this wrong, the process is broken. The process pits people against each other, and makes it harder to come out the other side with a good relationship and able to co-parent your kids successfully."'

Kate retrained as a family consultant, and started helping other couples going through divorce to avoid having the same problems as her. What she was doing was great, but it needed technology and a different approach to be able to scale it, and to have something that could help people across the country, or potentially across the world.

'It's a very personal thing, going through a divorce, and most people need a bit more help than you might be able to get with a purely technical solution. So, we launched a product that helps couples with a mixture of a divorce coach who acts as that middle person to get couples to the conclusion, plus technology to streamline the process, keep the costs as low as possible, and make the service accessible from anywhere in the country.

Over the years, we've proved without a doubt that we really do have a solution that works for people, with significant month-on-month growth and outstanding customer reviews. The fact that 'no-fault divorce' in the UK is imminent means that we are now absolutely poised to capitalise on this massive change in the market, which makes us very investable.'*

---

* Since this interview, no-fault divorce passed into law in England and Wales on 6 April 2022 as part of the Divorce, Dissolution and Separation Act 2020.

Competitive advantage

How is your solution better than anything else on the market?

Investors want to back winners, and love nothing more than being part of a business that creates and dominates a market. Your business must be clearly differentiated to be investable. What's your Unique Selling Point (USP) that makes your product or service stand head and shoulders above your competitors, and become the choice of preference for your target customers?

How will you stay ahead of the competition? Is your sustainable advantage because of some intellectual property, patent, know-how, first-to-market advantage, special skills and experience, brand loyalty or uniqueness that's hard to replicate?

Be clear on what uniquely gives your business the potential to win in your market:

- Pull together a full competitor analysis, to show how you stack up against other players in the field, in a simple spreadsheet.
- Focus not only on the features of each solution, but also the benefits.
- The list of comparables will be bespoke to your market: think about what drives a customer's decision to purchase one solution over another.
- Update this regularly: the last thing you want is an investor pointing out a competitor that you're not aware of, as this will really put you on the back foot.

Here's a simple example to get you started (Table 2).

Table 2: Competitor analysis

Features/ benefits	How it solves the problem	Best feature	Price point	Support levels	Branding	Disadvantages
My company						
Competitor 1						
Competitor 2						
Competitor 3						

STORY: A NOT SO TERRIBLE BUSINESS

Tersha Willis, terrible*

Tersha's background as a creative director for a streetwear brand – along with her co-founder Jack's experience in the music industry – led them to spot an opportunity to rectify the problems around merchandise in the music industry, and in 2016 they founded terrible*.

The company's out-of-the-box merchandise solution, using the latest technology and production capabilities, enables creators to design, make, deliver, license and sell products to their fans, generating an important revenue stream for them. Tersha raised £378,500 from private angel investors over two separate rounds.

> *'What's different about terrible* is that we provide the whole merchandise package to our clients: it's a full-service solution. We don't just help creators design and make high-quality merchandise, we help them sell it too, and provide unrivalled technology through our platform so they can track and manage their sales. Other players in the market only solve part of the problem.*
>
> *terrible* is blowing away the expectations of our customers, and shaking up the industry. We're super clear about which*

problem we are solving, and who our customer is. We focus on creators – and the largest segment of those creators are in the music industry. They don't have the time, skills or resources to develop a robust merchandise business on their own, but they need the revenue it generates.'

Business model

How does your company make money?

An investable business is one that can clearly demonstrate how it can be commercially viable, which goes way beyond simply outlining your pricing structure. Whether you're generating income from product or service sales, advertising, commission, subscriptions or any other route, what's important is demonstrating that you can make a profit.

Get clear on your business model, as you'll need to explain this to investors: one of the biases that female founders face is an assumption that we aren't strong on numbers – so prove them wrong!

We'll be covering this in more detail in Step 2 of the fundraising process (Chapter 6), but here are the top line numbers you'll need to communicate on your business model.

Basic unit economics

- What's the price of your product or service?
- What does it cost you to make or deliver?
- How much profit per unit do you make?
- How much do you need to sell to cover your overheads and break even (where your revenue covers all your costs, and you start to make a profit)?

Show you can make a good margin, and that break-even is possible within a reasonable time frame.

Customer value

This is how much a customer spends over the months or years they stay with you.

The lifetime value of a customer is calculated as follows:

Average Order Value x Purchases Per Year x Customer Lifespan in Years

= Lifetime Value

Marketing effectiveness

- What does it cost you to acquire a customer?
- How does this compare to the lifetime value of that customer?

Show that your marketing costs are a lot lower than the revenue and profit you can make from each customer over time.

Customer

What do you know about the customers you're targeting?

An investable company is one that understands its customers inside-out. When you know your customers well, investors feel more confident that you'll design solutions that solve those customers' problems, and that you know how to connect and convert your prospects.

Your early customer targets are likely to be those suffering most with the problem you've identified, have the highest propensity to buy, and who are easiest to reach. Develop customer profiles to show your understanding of the key people you plan to sell to: you may need to undertake some research in your market to get clarity on this.

These customer profiles (or 'avatars') for each of your target customer segments may include:

- **demographics** – their age, gender, marital status, education, employment and where they live
- **psychographics** – how their lives look on a typical day, week or year, what they're interested in, what their goals and values are, what brands they're interested in, what keeps them up at night
- **influences** – how they make their buying decisions, where they get their information, what media they consume.

Route to market

How will you reach your customers?

You can have the best business concept in the world, but if you can't communicate with and convert your target customers in a cost-effective way, it's going to be tricky for you to scale:

- What sales and marketing channels do you plan to use – for example, social media marketing, PR, mail order, trade shows, outdoor advertising, direct sales, retail distribution, wholesale?
- Why and what data do you have about how you expect each of these channels to perform?

Investors will be keen to understand this, particularly if you're raising money to spend on marketing, which is often the case for a start-up. They want to know that the investment will be deployed into activity that generates returns.

Traction

How much progress have you already made with the business, and how is that progress speeding up?

As we touched on in Chapter 3, the more you can show traction and momentum, the more you de-risk the investment opportunity. Demonstrating that you've found product-to-market fit with your product or service proves that people want what you're offering, and shows a firm foundation on which you can scale your business.

Above all, be proud and confident in what you've achieved!

How to measure traction

Which Key Performance Indicators (KPIs) are relevant for you to track to prove your traction in the market, depends largely on the key drivers that underpin the growth of your business.

One of the most important measures of traction is *revenue*: nothing proves that people want what you're offering more than putting their hand in their pocket to pay for it. But there are many other key data points that might be pertinent for your business, both quantitative and qualitative.

Quantitative measures

Here are just a few examples of metrics that may be relevant for you to track:

- revenue
- gross and net profit margins
- number of customers
- size of audience
- social media followers
- average order value – i.e. how much a customer spends per transaction
- annual revenue per customer

- Customer Lifetime Value
- website visits
- number of downloads
- frequency of website visits
- time spent on website
- conversion rate from initial lead through to sale
- Cost Per Acquisition (CPA) – i.e. how much it costs to acquire a customer
- customer satisfaction scores
- quality control measures
- speed of delivery.

KPIs that are improving month-on-month, quarter-on-quarter, year-on-year will help with your investment story, as this momentum shows your business is starting to take off.

Qualitative measures
A few examples of qualitative signs of your progress are:

- positive press coverage
- quotes from influential people in your industry
- customer testimonials
- celebrity endorsements
- industry awards.

Other indicators of traction can be key elements of your business operation that are locked in place and act as a defence against competitors, for example:

- trademarks
- intellectual property
- key team members
- exclusive partnerships
- suppliers or distributors you've secured.

How much traction is enough to interest investors?
This question is the holy grail of the start-up world – and there is no single answer, as it depends on the investor and the level of risk they're prepared to take.

Remember, given that you are one of the biggest, if not the only, investor in your business to date, what measures would *you* want to see before you feel confident that you're proving product-to-market fit?

Team

Do you have the right people in place to enable you to execute on your plan?

Many solo female founders worry that investors prefer a founding team of two or more. This isn't the case, as long as you can demonstrate that you have the skills and experience within your team to make your business a success.

You'll know better than anyone else what needs to be in place, because this is your business – but investors will want to see how you're addressing the following areas:

- **Leadership** – the entrepreneurial and leadership skills to take your business idea from seed stage through to growth.
- **Industry knowledge** – the requisite knowledge, experience and connections required within your market.

- **Technology** – strong technology skills to develop product and IT, and for operational management.
- **Operations** – the necessary logistics, production and customer service expertise to deliver the plan.
- **Sales and marketing** – the talent to reach and convert your customers, which may include business-to-business sales, retail experience, social media marketing and PR.
- **Finance** – strong day-to-day financial management, strategic financial support, professional bookkeeping and accounting.
- **Legal** – reputable and competent legal support to act for you through the investment deal itself, and on any other key legal issues as the company grows.

These skills and roles don't have to be filled by full-time employees; you might use external agencies or freelance staff. It also can be hugely valuable to have advisors who bring senior-level expertise and experience to support you in growing the business, with strategic advice and connections.

If there are gaps in your team's skills and experience, consider how you can fill them – if not now, then once you've raised investment. If you have individuals already identified to fill those roles, that strengthens your proposition.

The promise

What you are going to do in the future to scale this business, and create amazing outcomes for your investors?

There are three parts to this: road map, results and exit.

Road map

What are your top line plan and major milestones for taking the business to the next level over the next few years?

For example, will you:

- take on new team members
- fund new marketing activity
- develop your technology
- launch new products
- invest in stock
- put new operational systems in place
- expand into new geographical territories?

These major strategic initiatives need to be clearly outlined, along with timescales to execute.

Results

How do you expect your KPIs to improve as you implement your plans for growth?

For example:

- How will your customer base increase over the years?
- How will your customer acquisition costs and gross margins improve over time?
- How will your revenue and profit grow?

Investors will be looking for exponential growth in all your numbers.

(We'll look at how you build numbers into your financial forecasts in Step 2 [Chapter 6], as investors will want to see these details.)

Exit

What are the likely routes to sell your business in the future, so investors can achieve the returns they're seeking?

You might not have worked this out in detail just yet, but giving investors a sense of what the exit might look like, and being ambitious about that, gives them more confidence – remembering the principle that they'll be looking for a 10x return on investment or more.

If you think you might aim for a trade sale, what kind of organisation would be interested in buying your company, and why? Where possible, reference other similar companies which have exited, with details of the deals done, as this helps you and your investors understand the appetite for acquisition in your sector.

STORY: RESTORATION PLANS

Vanessa Jacobs, The Restory

The Restory is a B2C and B2B global aftercare platform whose clients include Farfetch, Manolo Blahnik, Selfridges and Harrods, among others. In 2017, Vanessa raised her first investment round to hire who would become her first co-founder and figure out a path to growing her business.

> *'I knew that for my company to be interesting to investors, I'd need a solid plan on how any funds would be used, what milestones I thought could be achieved in what time frame, and what metrics I would use to measure success.*
>
> *I knew the long-term plan was to build a reputation for excellence among consumers, use our reputation to expand into retailers, and then expand into "powering" aftercare for large fashion brands. But I needed to break this down step-by-step – at least as far as I reasonably could into the future.*

First, I needed a "growth engine" [proven methods of growth through sales and marketing activities], then I needed some additional staff and technology partners to help me scale operations; and all the while I needed to be scaling my capacity through more trade partners. I had a plan for where I needed to spend extra money in the business in the short to medium term, and had a pretty good idea of the results this would bring.

There were three major areas that I wanted to focus on. The priority was growth: we focused on direct mail and Pay Per Click advertising on Google. The second was operations: I hired two people to process items and service clients. The third was technology: I hired a New York/New Delhi agency (owned by a friend of one of my first investors and advisors) to build our first order management system.

All of this was laid out in a five-year plan (that in some ways has held true over the years), and it gave me, my investors and my new fledgling team confidence in the general shape of the business, how we would make money, and how the business would reach its goals.

All this planning was a lot of work, and there is a balance between looking at trends and envisioning the future and focusing on what is right in front of you – but it made it so clear to me that the business did have a big enough market, and therefore potential.

Once I'd convinced myself The Restory was an exciting opportunity, I knew I'd be able to convince external investors too.'

Due diligence

Is your company paperwork in order, and can you prove all the things about your business that you're asserting?

Before an investor puts their money into your company, they will want to check that your start-up is in good shape from a compliance and risk management perspective.

These checks won't happen until you have a deal on the table, but it's worth getting everything organised sooner rather than later, so that you aren't tripped up further on:

- Ensure all your statutory company filings are up-to-date.
- Check all company accounts are filed, management accounts are current and all taxes paid.
- Get contracts in place with all your suppliers, partners and staff, and for any property owned or leased.
- Ensure there are thorough records on customers and orders.
- Verify KPIs.
- Formalise details of any loans into the company, including money that founders or friends and family might have put into it.
- Register any intellectual property or trademarks in the business.

All this information should be filed digitally and stored securely in one place, called a 'data room' – ideally in the cloud, so it can be easily shared with interested investors. This will make your life so much less painful in getting your investment deal over the line.

Now we've covered all the fundamentals on your business that investors need to know, let's move on to the next step, where we'll look at how to translate your plan into a financial forecast, and how to structure your investment deal to take to market.

Action steps

Make sure you can answer the following questions about your business:

1. What's the ultimate vision for my business?
2. What's the problem my customers are experiencing, why is this is a serious problem for them, and how do I know this?
3. How big is the size of the opportunity, is it growing, and what data do I have to back this up?
4. Why is now the right time for my start-up to make an impact in the market?
5. What are the top three ways that my solution solves the problem, and the tangible benefits for our customers?
6. How is my solution better than anything else on the market, and how will I maintain my competitive lead?
7. Who are my primary target customers, why is this segment attractive, and what other customers might I target as we grow?
8. What's my commercial model: how do I price my product or service, do my unit economics stack up, and can I profitably acquire customers?
9. How will I reach my customers, and why is this the fastest and/or most effective way?

10. How am I already proving that my solution is a great fit for this market, and what evidence do I have that my business is taking off?
11. Why is my team the best in the world to take this business forward, and how does each person add value and help me achieve successful outcomes for the business?
12. What are my major plans in the short, medium and long term that will enable me to grow the business?
13. How do I think my company will grow over the next three to five years in terms of number of customers, revenue and other important measures of business success?
14. How might I exit my business, and why?
15. Is all my company paperwork in order, and do I have a good lawyer on board?

6
Step 2: Commercials

As an entrepreneurial leader, it's critical that you have a handle on your numbers – and never more so than when raising investment. We know that women hold back from asking for funding if they're not confident with their financial skills,[1] and often come under more scrutiny on their financials too.[2]

You don't need to be a financial expert, but you do need to know what drives the performance and growth of your business, and to be able to structure your investment deal. You also need enough financial literacy to be able to hold your own in a conversation with an investor, otherwise it's unlikely they're going to trust you with their money.

We'll cover the Commercial essentials in here in Step 2 of the fundraising process.

Build your financial forecast

Your financial forecast is a spreadsheet that has the details of what you project your revenue, costs, profits, cash flow and balance sheet to be, usually for the next three to five years. Investors will want to see your summary financial forecast, and many will go into detail with you on the numbers, so they can really understand both the opportunity in front of them and your capabilities as an entrepreneur.

Your forecast serves you in two ways.

Demonstrates the business and investment opportunity

Your financial forecast enables both you and your investor to understand that:

- the market you plan to capture is large enough, and there is potential to achieve significant growth in customers and revenue
- customers can be reached in a cost-effective way
- your business operations can be run at a reasonable cost
- your product or service can be sold at a profit, and gross margins meet or exceed industry benchmarks
- break-even can be achieved within a reasonable time frame – or if you're pushing for growth over profitability, that the plan on how to finance any shortfalls is clear, to minimise the risk of running out of cash
- there is a clear plan on how investment funds will be deployed to grow the business and generate greater revenue, profit and, ultimately, value over time.

Demonstrates your personal capabilities

Your financial forecast, along with the discussions you have with an investor on your financials, provides them with great insight on you as the founder, to assess whether you:

- know how to financially manage your business

- have the industry and functional skills and experience to make realistic assumptions and goals
- aim to continuously improve the efficiency of your business as it grows
- understand the importance of cash management and planning your investment journey
- recognise there may be challenges along the way, and have stress-tested your forecasts.

How to build your financial model

A financial model is the spreadsheet template used to create a financial forecast. If you're not familiar with working with spreadsheets like Excel, take a short online course to master the basics and increase your confidence in working with numbers.

A good financial model should:

- be broken out into as much granular detail as possible – ideally on a month-by-month basis
- use different worksheets – for profit and loss, cash flow, balance sheet, historic data, assumptions and staff headcount
- include historic data on previous performance – as a benchmark for forecast data
- be built using logic and formulas – so when assumptions change, the forecast automatically updates, making it easy to test different variables in the plan
- have clear colour coding – to show where to input data and key assumptions

- include tables and charts – to summarise headline data, so that expected results and trends can be assessed immediately.

There are several ways to build your model.

Customise a basic financial model template

A simple online search for 'financial model template' will deliver many results: some will be free, while others are paid.

You'll need to adapt the template to make it work for your business; but if you have extremely limited budgets and enough expertise with spreadsheets, this may be adequate for a first funding round. (You'll find a few examples in the Further Resources to get you started.)

Use an online financial model service

Online tools (some examples of which you'll find in the Further Resources) are fairly easy to use, with nicely designed reports and charts as standard – but they can be limited in terms of customisation to meet your needs. They are usually priced on a low-cost, monthly fee basis, so will keep your costs down.

Have your own financial model built

A good accountant or a freelance financial modeller who understands start-ups and finance-raising can create a custom model for you, based on the key assumptions you provide.

This solution is more expensive – you might expect to pay up to a few thousand pounds – but it's my preferred solution for clients because a robust model will be an invaluable tool over several years, and an investment that really pays off.

A financial forecast model is complex and as such, challenging to provide examples of them within a book. Here are some examples of the key output tables and graphs you will need to produce (Tables 3 and 4, and Figures 4 and 5).

Table 3: Example of five-year forecast summary

Year ending 31 December	2021 Actual £	2022 Budget £	2023 Forecast £	2024 Forecast £	2025 Forecast £	2026 Forecast £	2027 Forecast £
Revenue							
Product A	86,000	172,000	344,000	688,000	1,376,000	2,752,000	5,504,000
Product B		18,000	100,000	200,000	400,000	800,000	100,000
Product C				150,000	180,000	250,000	400,000
TOTAL	86,000	190,000	444,000	1,038,000	1,956,000	3,802,000	6,004,000
Cost of goods sold	43,000	89,300	199,800	435,960	782,400	1,482,780	2,281,520
Gross profit	43,000	100,700	244,200	602,040	1,173,600	2,319,220	3,722,480
Gross profit margin	50%	53%	55%	58%	60%	61%	62%
Operating expenses							
Payroll	0	120,000	250,000	325,000	450,000	500,000	625,000
Marketing	30,000	50,000	100,000	120,000	200,000	400,000	500,000
Technology	10,000	30,000	100,000	100,000	180,000	200,000	200,000
Facilities	6,000	7,000	10,000	20,000	25,000	30,000	35,000
Professional services	6,000	6,000	6,000	12,000	12,000	12,000	24,000
TOTAL	52,000	213,000	466,000	577,000	867,000	1,142,000	1,384,000
Net profit	-9,000	-112,300	-221,800	25,040	306,600	1,177,220	2,338,480
Net profit margin	-10%	-59%	-50%	2%	16%	31%	39%
Investment	125,000		250,000				
Cash balance	116,000	3,700	31,900	56,940	363,540	1,540,760	3,879,240

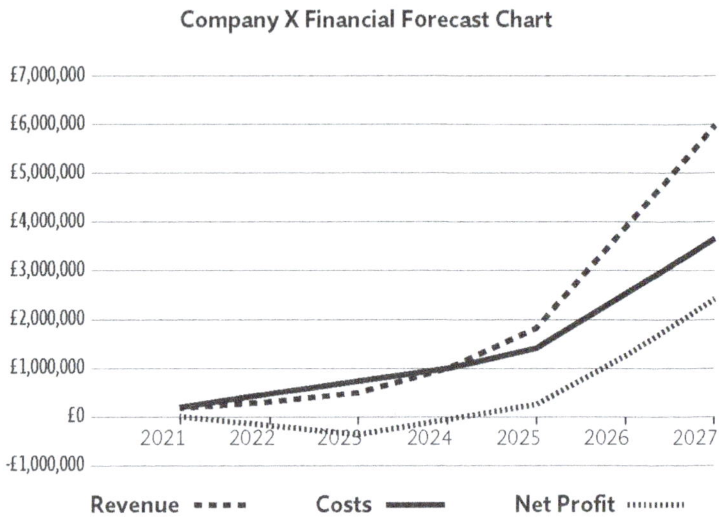

Figure 4: Example of key financials graph

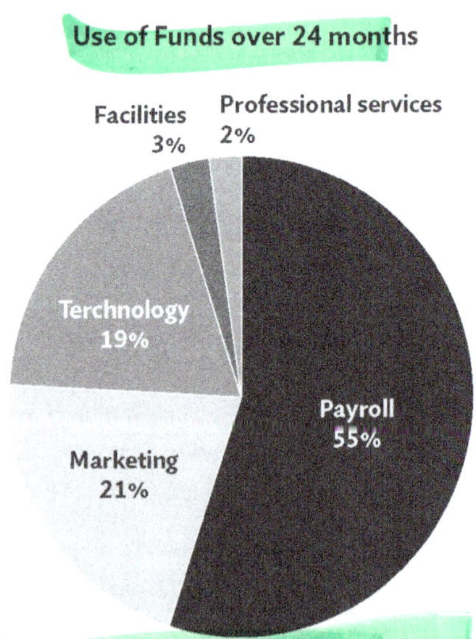

Figure 5: Example of use of funds pie chart

Table 4: Example of Key Performance Indicators summary table

	2021	2022	2023	2024	2025	2026	2027
New customers	5,000	10,000	20,000	30,000	50,000	120,000	180,000
Cost per acquisition	£6.00	£5.00	£5.00	£4.00	£4.00	£3.33	£2.78
TOTAL CUSTOMERS	5,000	15,000	35,000	65,000	115,000	235,000	415,000
Average revenue per customer	£17.20	£12.67	£12.69	£15.97	£17.01	£16.18	£14.47
Marketing cost as % of sales	35%	26%	23%	12%	10%	11%	8%
New customers	5,000	10,000	20,000	30,000	50,000	120,000	180,000
Cost per acquisition	£6.00	£5.00	£5.00	£4.00	£4.00	£3.33	£2.78
TOTAL CUSTOMERS	5,000	15,000	35,000	65,000	115,000	235,000	415,000
Average revenue per customer	£17.20	£12.67	£12.69	£15.97	£17.01	£16.18	£14.47
Marketing cost as % of sales	35%	26%	23%	12%	10%	11%	8%

Financial support

Expert financial support is essential for any start-up business that's pushing for high growth, both to ensure you're meeting statutory requirements around bookkeeping, tax and year-end accounts, but also from a financial management and planning perspective.

This expertise doesn't need to be in-house, especially in the early days: as mentioned previously in Step 1, professional support can be freelance, virtual or part-time. What's important is that your finance expert helps you to own and understand your own financials because at the end of the day, you're the one who's going to sit with investors and explain your numbers – you can't outsource that bit.

STORY: HEALTHY FOOD AND HEALTHY FINANCIALS

Kristina Komlosiova and Stephanie Johnson, Pollen + Grace

Pollen + Grace is a natural food company with a delicious range of home-cooked ready meals and snacks free from gluten, wheat and dairy.

Since its launch in late 2015, the business has grown exponentially: Pollen + Grace is now stocked in places such as Sainsbury's, Tesco, Co-op, Ocado, WHSmith, Amazon Fresh and Wholefoods.

Self-funded for the first 18 months, Kristina and Stephanie went on to raise £3.5 million across multiple funding rounds from angel investors, a family office (a private firm that actively manages a family's or individual's wealth – more on this in Chapter 8), crowdfunding and a VC syndicate. This helped them on their way to achieving their mission to become the most trusted healthy food brand in the UK, and change the way the nation eats for the better.

> *'Finance is the single most important part that you need as a business, to be able to talk to investors and attract investment. If you don't know the finances of your business, you don't really know your business or how you're going to progress it to the next level.*
>
> *Neither of us comes from a finance background, so we had a virtual finance director [FD] from pretty much day one. He set up everything for us in terms of management accounts, how*

we report everything and our financial model, and we learned from him along the way.

We remember the very first time when we were talking to him and he was showing us his spreadsheets on the screen, and we were like: "Oh my goodness, we can't follow anything!" But although he set up elaborate and complex systems for us, he explained everything to us, and we learned so much from him – and that's been incredible.

Now we're on a level where we can create our forecasts ourselves: we can pretty much do anything, he just checks them. It was a lot of education and a huge learning curve for both of us. Our FD is still working with us to this day – he's still virtual, he's still part-time.'

Work out your assumptions

Once you've got your financial model, you can start filling it in with your assumptions on what you think will happen with your business.

Before you input numbers into the model itself, make a note of your assumptions in a simple Word document. This helps you remember what you were thinking, as it can be hard to unpick your assumptions if all you do is type in the numbers directly into a spreadsheet.

Expenses (overheads and fixed costs)

List all the items you'll need to spend money on, which aren't directly related to how much product or service you sell. This includes, for example:

- office costs
- technology

- travel
- admin
- staff
- marketing.

Work off the basis of what you're spending now, and look at how you expect you'll need to increase each of these costs as the business grows:

- Will they go up gradually each month?
- Will there be a step-change at a certain point – e.g. in month 2 you want to invest in a new website; in month 12 you plan to move into a larger office; in month 20 you anticipate launching a new product line, etc.

Detail staff headcount into roles, salaries and when you expect to take on each person.

Break down marketing costs as much as possible, to show you clearly understand the costs and effectiveness of the marketing activity you do. For example, if you're an e-commerce business planning to start spending £5,000 a month on social media advertising:

- What cost per click do you expect?
- How many visitors to your website will that translate into?
- What conversion rate from visit to sale would you expect?

In the model, this can be directly linked to your e-commerce revenue.

Don't forget to put in the costs of your anticipated fundraise. It's wise to allow:

- 7 per cent for investment platform charges (paid following the raise)
- a few thousand pounds for legal fees
- a few thousand pounds for engaged professional support to help you prepare for and run your campaign.

Revenue (turnover)

Think about what drives your revenue and break it down as much as possible. For example, if you're an online business, show website traffic, conversion rates and average order value – your revenue will be a multiplication of all three numbers.

If you're selling to businesses (B2B), show:

No. of Customers x No. of Products x Average Order Value

– to derive your revenue.

If it makes sense, break down your revenue by customer type or product line. Again, the more granular you can get, the better – as this helps you and your investors see how the forecasts have been put together.

Consider how your customer growth and revenue link to your sales and marketing activities. These should be connected in your financial model using formulas, where possible.

Cost of goods sold

What costs do you incur every time you sell a product or service? This might include:

- raw materials
- packaging
- logistics

- credit card fees
- delivery, etc.

Break them out as much as you can.

Sense-checking

Once you have assumptions in your model, it's important to go back and sense-check them.

- Do your overheads need to increase as your revenue increases? For example, is there a point where you'll have so many staff that you need new office space, or volume sales that require you to take on extra customer service staff or new warehousing facilities?
- Check your key ratios, such as gross and net margin, to make sure they're healthy – and, ideally, showing improvements over time.
- Can you see a point where you'll reach break-even? Note when this is, and how many sales or clients you need to get to achieve it.
- Check your annual summaries – how do the numbers progress over the years: do they lift steadily, do you see big jumps, do you feel they're realistic? How are you achieving growth, and have you got the costs in the model that support it?

Scenario planning

Consider how things might look if your growth plans don't go as well as you are hoping; and on the flip side, what the business might look like if things go much better than anticipated. Save different versions of your financial model based on the best and worst cases, for example:

- What happens if you improve your conversion rates by 20 per cent?
- What's the impact if you change your price?
- What happens if your costs go up by 30 per cent?
- What if you launch that second product line six months later?

This helps you both to prepare for different outcomes, and to answer investor questions about how you'll manage risk.

Determine your raise amount

Typically, female founders don't raise as much money as male founders on an investment round. On average, we estimate that we need 40 per cent less funding to launch our business, and we start them with 53 per cent less capital than men.

In 2019, female-led start-ups raised an average of £514,000 compared with £1.4 million for mixed gender-led companies, and £1.8 million by all-male teams.[3] This is partly explained by the fact that more women-led businesses are at an earlier stage, and there have been some mega-deals at later stage by businesses founded by men.

However, there is also truth in the fact that women don't like to ask for what they see as 'too much'.

As we've seen in previous chapters, the danger of not asking for enough investment is running out of money far more quickly than we might realise, which can really hold back growth and land us back in another funding round far sooner than anticipated. What seems like a huge amount of money when we first receive it from investors will slip through our fingers like water, once we start employing it into our cash-hungry start-up.

We optimistic entrepreneurs often forget that everything usually takes twice as long, and costs twice as much, as we think it will.

However, there is also danger in raising too much investment! Rolling in the money can make an entrepreneur a little less careful with spending, and a little less mindful about getting a good return on those funds. Plus, of course, we must factor in the valuation of our business, as the amount we raise needs to be assessed in relation to this, to determine how much equity we'll offer to investors. Raising a lot of money against a low valuation in the early days means ending up selling a more significant share of the business than might be necessary. (We'll look at valuation in more detail in the next section of this chapter.)

How to work out the cash you need

- Review your cash forecast over the next 12–18 months, and look at where you have the largest negative amount. That will tell you your likely cash shortfall.
- Work out your 'burn rate' – i.e. how much money you spend each month on fixed costs, even if you don't generate sales revenue.
- Add in a contingency amount that would cover four to six months of burn rate. This extra money should give you a safety net for things not going to plan, and a longer 'runway' (i.e. number of months before the money runs out) to raise your next investment round, if you need it.

For example, if the cash shortfall in your 18-month forecast is £190,000, and your burn rate over six months is £10,000 per month, you might want to raise £190,000 + £60,000 = £250,000.

Once you've worked out your ideal raise amount:

- Put the investment money into your cash flow worksheet. You should put this in for the month you expect your investment round to close (not forgetting that it typically takes four to six months to complete a fundraising campaign and get the money in the bank).

- If you expect further investment rounds to keep the business cash-positive over the years, then put them in the forecast for later dates.

Valuing your business

Putting a price on your business is one of the most challenging issues to figure out when you're a start-up, because there is no simple way of calculating it at the early stage. It's an art and a science, and that makes most of us nervous about getting it wrong. I can practically guarantee that everyone you ask will give you a different view on what your business valuation should be.

At the end of the day you're going to need to make that call, but you need to do this with due thought and process, rather than just sticking your finger in the air.

If an accountant were to look at the *actual* value of your business right now, the number they'd come up with would probably be tiny. They would look at the value of the assets you have, factor in the revenue and profits, consider the investment that's gone into the business to date, what it might cost someone else to build the business, and make a calculation. The reality for most start-ups is that they have very few assets, are turning over very little and rarely making a profit, so the accounting 'book value' comes out at zero, or not much more.

High-growth potential start-ups tend to be valued on their *potential*: the vision of the business you're building, and its anticipated value and impact. Ultimately, your business is only worth what someone is prepared to pay for it: value your business too low, and you sell yourself short; value it too high, and you risk not securing investment at all.

And in both scenarios, there is the fear of humiliation or failure.

This fear of failure, as discussed in Chapter 4 on fundraising mindset, can be a real issue for female founders. Unfortunately, we often undervalue not only ourselves, but also our businesses. Data show that at 'seed' stage (in the early days, while we're proving the business concept) we value our companies 30 per cent lower than all-male or mixed teams value theirs; a disparity that increases to 40 per cent at venture stage (when we're starting to scale), and a whopping 59 per cent at growth stage (when we start to expand a proven business)[4] (Figure 6).

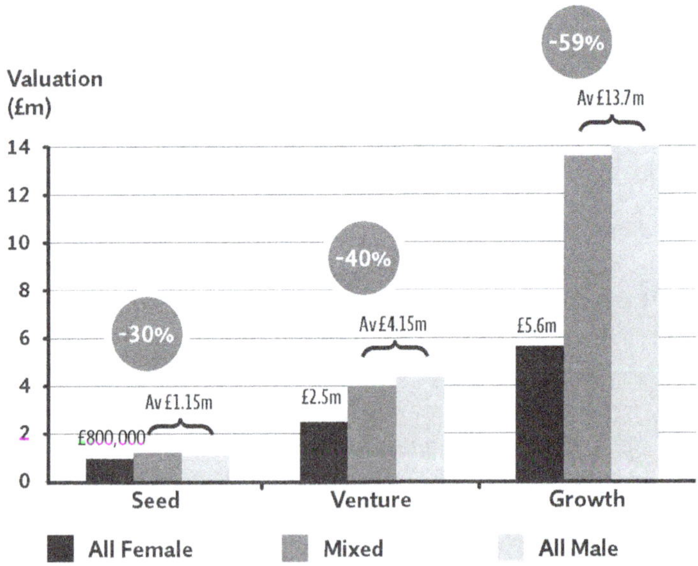

Figure 6: Start-up valuations at different stages, based on gender of founding team

Source: Beauhurst (2019) (Data reproduced with kind permission)

This undervaluation can lead to real problems for female founders, as we scale our companies. If we value our business too low at the start, then as we raise investment for growth, we end up retaining less ownership of our company than we should. This can give investors more control and influence – ultimately, when we scale and exit the business, we're left with way less than we should have.

It might feel a little uncomfortable for you to think about your business being worth a six-figure sum now, when you're only at the start of your journey. But valuation is simply a paper-based number – it's not actual money in your pocket until you exit the business – so, focus on your overall long-term goal and be ambitious in setting your value.

Bear in mind that once investors have shown an interest in your company, you may need to negotiate your valuation with them – so it's better to start with a valuation a little higher than you're hoping for, to leave yourself some wiggle room. (I've yet to meet an investor who has negotiated the value of a start-up in the upward direction!)

It's not easy trying to figure out your valuation, and almost impossible to know if you've got it anywhere near right until you look back in years to come and deconstruct it. But you owe it to yourself to do your best to build the case for a strong valuation, and it's advisable to get professional support on this.

How to get the best valuation

Benchmarking

As we've seen, although it's important to be ambitious about your valuation, that doesn't mean you can just make something up without justifying it – you need to be in the right ballpark.

Here are the typical valuation ranges we tend to see, depending on the stage of the business, which can be a helpful starting place (Table 5).

Table 5: Typical valuation ranges by stage of business[5]

Stage	Valuation
Idea	£300,000–£500,000
Development	£300,000–£750,000
Launch	£500,000–£1 million
Traction	£1–£2 million
Revenue	£1–£3 million
Scale	£3 million+

Source: Seed Legals (2019)

It's also vital to research valuations for comparable businesses: those in the same industry as you or with similar business models. Go to Crunchbase.com, check out public crowdfunding websites and research news online to see what similar companies to yours have been valued at along their life cycle and through to exit, if that has happened.

Are you operating in a 'hot' sector? Where you are on the market trend curve will have an impact on whether you can push your valuation up – so, research what the investment community is saying about your industry, to inform your valuation decision and provide extra justification to investors on the price you want to set.

Ownership structure

Founders often ask how much equity they should give away. The simple answer to that question is: absolutely nothing! It's quite baffling why the start-up industry uses this phrasing, because you never 'give away' equity; instead, you exchange it in return for something of value – and in the case of investment, that value is cash. Your valuation, coupled with the amount you raise, is what determines the equity on offer to investors.

Let's look at how this is calculated, based on an example of raising £250,000 on a valuation of £1 million (Table 6).

Table 6: Calculating equity on offer

A	Pre-Money Valuation	The company valuation *before* you've raised investment	£1,000,000
B	Raise Amount	The amount of investment you're seeking	£250,000
C	Post-Money Valuation (A+B)	The company valuation *after* you've raised investment	£1,250,000
D	Equity Offered (B÷C)	The percentage of your company that you will exchange for the investment	20%

In this example, you've sold 20 per cent of the company. Assuming this is the first time you've raised investment, that means you still own 80 per cent of the business, leaving you plenty of scope to raise more investment later and still retain majority ownership.

A high-growth potential business might expect to sell between 16 and 25 per cent of equity during the seed funding phase. The average start-up raises £2 million in seed funding before they're ready for Series A, and it's very common that this early-stage funding comes in multiple investment rounds.

Ideally, your valuation should improve over time as you achieve key milestones and build more value, further de-risking the investment opportunity (Figure 7):

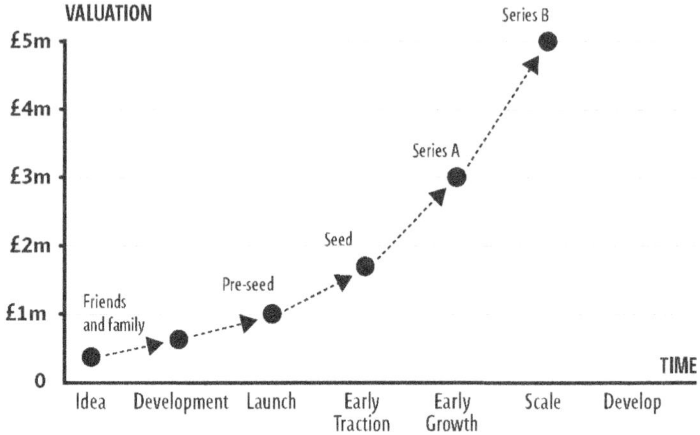

Figure 7: Valuation progression over time

Be careful not to overinflate your valuation just to make the maths work. For example, if you need to raise £1 million now, but you want to ensure you don't sell more than 25 per cent of the business, you'll need a valuation of £3 million, calculated as follows (Table 7).

Table 7: Calculating Pre-Money Valuation based on the equity you wish to offer

A	Pre-Money Valuation (C-B)	The company valuation *before* you've raised investment	£3,000,000
B	Raise Amount	The amount of investment you're seeking	£1,000,000
C	Post-Money Valuation (B÷D)	The company valuation *after* you've raised investment	£4,000,000
D	Equity Offered	The percentage of your company that you will exchange for the investment	25%

$$\text{Post-Money Valuation} = \text{Raise Amount} \div \text{Equity Offered}$$

$$= £1{,}000{,}000 \div 25\%$$

$$= £4{,}000{,}000$$

$$\text{Pre-Money Valuation} = \text{Post-Money Valuation} - \text{Raise Amount}$$

$$= £4{,}000{,}000 - £1{,}000{,}000$$

$$= £3{,}000{,}000$$

If a £3 million valuation isn't commensurate with your stage of business or comparable companies in the industry – or truly justifiable, given your investment proposal – you're probably going to struggle. You may need to phase the amount you raise into smaller tranches, with the view that on subsequent investment rounds you'll be able to push that valuation up, and ultimately sell less equity.

The danger is that if you don't deliver results for investors on future investment rounds, your valuation may be cut significantly, because investors aren't convinced that your company is worth as much as you were projecting. This is called a 'down-round': it never looks good for a start-up, and can be a risk if you overvalue your company (Figure 8).

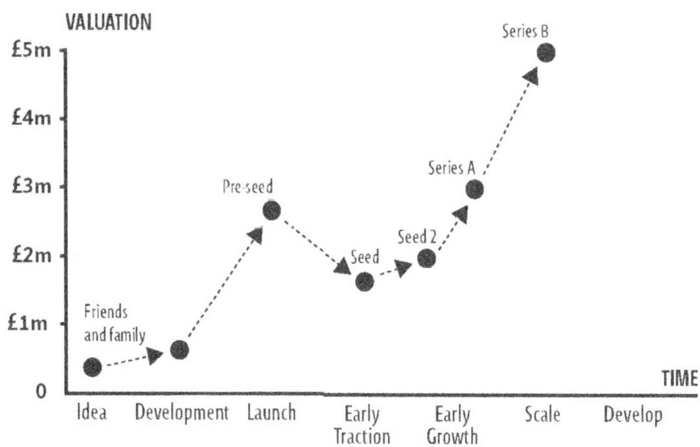

Figure 8: A down-round on valuation

The trick is to find that 'Goldilocks' valuation that's not too much and not too little, but just right: that properly values what you have to offer. And remember, although your personal share of the business will get smaller as you dilute your ownership by bringing more investors on board, by using that investment to grow the overall value of the business, you'll own a smaller piece of a much bigger pie.

STORY: THE VALUE OF TOILET PAPER

Julie Chen, The Cheeky Panda

Julie and her then-fiancé (now husband) Chris were visiting her parents in China when they saw that 90 per cent of the bamboo crop, which can be harvested every year, was being wasted.

Knowing that 27,000 trees are chopped down every day in the UK to make toilet paper, they saw a huge opportunity to create a more conscious choice for consumers by using this alternative material. And so they created The Cheeky Panda: eco-friendly tissue paper and biodegradable wipes made from 100 per cent bamboo.

Julie started selling the product online via Amazon in 2016, and following strong sales and amazing customer reviews, traditional retailer interest followed.

The company grew exponentially, as did its valuation over just four short years as they raised each investment round, as follows:

Year	Method	Investment raised	Valuation	Equity sold
2016	Angels	£100,000	£900,000	10%
2016	Angels	£95,000	£1.9 million	5%
2018	Crowdfunding	£500,000	£5 million	9%
2019	Crowdfunding	£1.5 million	£25 million	5.5%
2020	Crowdfunding	£2.4 million	£52.6 million	4.4%†

In 2020, after five fundraising rounds and £4.6 million in funding, Julie and Chris still owned more than two-thirds of the business. Julie has been bold with her valuation at every step of the way:

> *'Toilet paper requires an intensive amount of capital. It's high-volume, low-margin, so funding is important to help us grow fast. We needed more stock and more people to help: we crowdfunded to get more people supporting us. But we don't want to develop the business and end up with just a small percentage of equity, which I've seen happen with other businesses – so we pushed for a high valuation.*
>
> *'We believe in our brand and our product. With the amount of trees and carbon saved by switching people to use bamboo, we are creating value for the world with our investors and customers. We've built a very engaging and loyal community using crowdfunding.'*

Deferring the valuation decision

You can defer valuing your company by raising money using an Advanced Subscription Agreement (ASA) in the UK, a Simple Agreement for Future Equity (SAFE) in the USA, or the internationally accepted Convertible Note, which can be a good

† The numbers here are calculated per the formula in Table 6: Calculating equity on offer.

option – especially in the early days when it's quite challenging to value your company.

These agreements, which are reasonably simple and fast to execute, enable investors to put money into your business now that converts into equity at a discount when you raise your next 'priced' investment round (with Convertible Notes, there is also the option to pay the money back as you would a loan).

With these agreements, you'll usually need to agree a valuation minimum and maximum for the point of conversion into equity – so you'll still need to make a broad decision on where you think your valuation might be.

Maximising your valuation

Building strengths in all five steps of raising investment is critical when it comes to achieving a strong valuation. A confident founder who not only has a great company and strong commercials, but who can communicate the opportunity well, connect with the right investors and secure their commitment through effective negotiations, will undoubtably achieve a far higher price for their business than a founder who hasn't mastered these skills.

You can benchmark your capabilities using my Female Founder Investability Scorecard™ (which you'll find in the Further Resources).

Project return on investment

Given that a major factor in valuing your start-up is its future potential, how do you know what your company might be worth years down the line? Unless you have a crystal ball or can travel through time, it's anyone's best guess! But it's helpful at the very least to have a sense for how things might pan out.

Your future valuation will be partly calculated based on the revenues and profits you expect to generate over the years; but it also can be highly influenced by the strategic value of your company, which goes way beyond its financial performance. Many companies are bought for the value of their data insights, customer database, brand, strategic partnerships or know-how and other key strategic assets.

In Step 1 we discussed the typical returns investors are looking for: 10x uplift over five to seven years. If your business is worth £1 million now, can you build it to be worth £10 million within the next five years or so, at the point where you can achieve an exit? If you're only expecting to increase the value of your company threefold within that time frame, most investors aren't going to be interested, because the risk–reward ratio is too high. Equally, if you're projecting a 50x return on investment, unless you have some pretty strong evidence to back that up, most investors are going to think that's an incredibly unrealistic expectation, and your credibility will be instantly undermined.

Being clear on the value you're building with your business beyond the balance sheet will help you convince investors on your projected future valuation, and why you expect to make such great returns for them.

Benefiting from the UK Enterprise Investment Schemes

If you're raising finance in the UK, you have a UK registered company (or a branch or subsidiary in the UK) and you're a UK resident, you may qualify for the Seed Enterprise Investment Scheme (SEIS) and/or the Enterprise Investment Scheme (EIS).

Early-stage investors are much more interested in those companies that qualify for SEIS/EIS, because they can get attractive tax breaks while supporting high-growth UK companies. In fact, 80 per cent of the total of UK angel investors' portfolio is in SEIS/EIS eligible businesses,[6] demonstrating just how important this is to them.

Some key benefits of the scheme are that investors:

- can claim back up to 50 per cent of their investment against income tax
- can offset any losses they make against capital gains or income tax
- don't have to pay capital gains tax when they sell their shares, if they've held them for at least three years
- don't have to pay any inheritance tax, if shares are held for at least two years.

Note that you must use any qualifying investment to grow the business through trading activity or investing in R&D; you can't use EIS funding to pay back loans. Employees, major shareholders and family members who invest in your business don't qualify for the scheme.

If you're raising money using an ASA, this can still be done within the SEIS/EIS investment scheme if your 'priced' investment round happens within six months.

Here are the key differences between the two schemes.

SEIS:

- focuses on very early-stage companies
- the business must have been trading for less than three years
- only the first £250,000 raised can qualify
- investors get a 50 per cent tax break
- investors can put in a maximum of £200,000 total per year into SEIS start-ups
- investors can't take more than a 30 per cent stake in the business to qualify.

EIS:

- designed with small and medium-sized businesses in mind
- the business must have been trading for less than seven years, or have raised some EIS funding within the first seven years
- the business can raise up to £5 million per year of EIS funding
- investors get a 30 per cent tax break
- investors can put in a maximum of £1 million total per year into EIS start-ups.

Do check all the latest rules and qualification criteria with HM Revenue & Customs (HMRC) (see Further Resources).

Most investors will want to see you have Advanced Assurance that you qualify for SEIS/EIS before they invest: this is a document which you can apply for from HMRC. You'll need to have all the information about your business (for example, your financial forecasts, along with your pitch deck, which we'll cover in Chapter 7) ready to send in with your application. It's possible to make this application yourself, although you may wish to get the support of your financial advisor if you feel your case might be complex, or want to be certain you'll get it all right.

Summarise your deal structure

Once you've pulled together your financial forecasts, raise amount and valuation, you have the fundamentals in place to formulate your ask for investors, which includes:

- **Raise amount** – how much investment you're seeking to grow the business.
- **Valuation** – the pre-money valuation of your company, before you've raised investment.
- **Equity on offer** – the calculation of how much of your business investors will own following the investment round.
- **Expected returns** – what return on investment you're projecting for investors, based on your plans for growth and company exit.
- **Tax breaks on offer** – whether your business qualifies for the UK SEIS/EIS scheme.
- **Use of funds** – a breakdown of how you intend to spend the investment.
- **Timescales** – when the investment round will be closing, which you should set as a few months before you need the cash into the business, to allow time to execute the paperwork and close the deal.

In Step 3 we'll look at how to communicate your company and commercial information effectively to investors, which is the final stage of preparing to launch your investment campaign.

Action steps

1. Make sure you have a good finance person on your team to support you in managing your financials and preparing your forecast for your investment campaign.
2. Decide what financial model you'll use: something bespoke that is built just for you, or a standard template.
3. Before you start populating your model, write out your assumptions on the revenue you expect to generate, the direct costs associated with delivering your product or service, and the overheads of running the business.
4. Once you've plugged the numbers into the model, check that the overall 'story' of the business makes sense: that your KPIs, growth projections and associated costs are ambitious enough, but also realistic, over three to five years.
5. Scenario plan for best and worst cases by changing your assumptions, and saving a few different versions of your plan.
6. Calculate how much you need to raise by looking at your cash flow requirements, plus a cash runway to leave you enough time to raise any further investment rounds you might need.
7. Assess what stage of business you are at as a starting point for calculating your valuation.
8. Research comparable valuations by searching online for similar start-up businesses that have funded or even exited, as another benchmark indicator.
9. Set yourself a target for what you believe your valuation could get to in five to seven years, based on your financial forecasts and the strategic value of the assets you're building.

he strength of your ability to raise investment using ale Founder Investability Scorecard: if you score ou can be more confident with your valuation.

11. Look at your cash flow projections to get a sense of how much funding you'll need along your start-up journey. Most high-growth potential businesses need consistent funding and increasingly large rounds to help them reach their potential.
12. Check your valuation against the amount of investment you need, understand the amount of equity you'll be offering investors, and ensure you're not selling too much of your business too soon.
13. If you qualify for the UK EIS/SEIS scheme, secure Advanced Assurance from HMRC.
14. Based on all the points above, make a call on the valuation you feel is right, and pull together your investment ask. Ideally, get professional support to stress-test this.

7
Step 3: Communication

Let me share a secret with you: investors won't read your business plan, because they simply don't have time to wade through a 40-page document, and don't need that level of detail. They're busy people and want to get to the nub of you, your business and your investment proposal as quickly as possible.

Telling your story effectively to an investor when you meet them – at a networking event, over an introductory email or social media message, or in a more formal meeting – is a critical skill to develop, which we'll cover here in Step 3 of the fundraising process.

The power of a story

Humans have been telling stories for centuries, we can't get enough of them. Stories transmit meaning and knowledge in an emotional way – because after all, we are emotional creatures. And if your story stimulates a positive emotional reaction, it will be more widely shared and embraced. Stories help you create a deeper connection and engagement with your audience, giving more meaning for them. They make you memorable, helping you stand out in a very competitive market – which is super important when you're raising investment.

People don't remember facts. They remember stories.

When communicating with investors, we want to take the listener on a journey: draw them in, create excitement, anticipation and intrigue, build up to a thrilling climax, followed by a satisfying conclusion. Help your audience use their imagination, so they feel what's going on in visceral way, and paint a picture in their mind that helps them relate to the story.

A relatable story is very powerful, as we are drawn to stories which have characters that look like us, or at least share characteristics to whom we can relate.

To be clear: by 'story', this doesn't mean you should make things up! Your business and investment story must be genuine and authentic, and indeed it's critical that the listener hears lots of evidence and facts throughout. Not only does this give credibility both to your story and you-as-storyteller, but it also allows the listener to bring their own personal meaning to the narrative, providing them with the space to make their own opinions and interpretations. When the listener brings their experiences to the story, it creates deeper meaning for them and a deeper bond: this is called 'neural coupling'.

Told well, your story will magnetise your investor – and if the fit is right, leave them feeling compelled to back you.

Craft your investment narrative

With storytelling in mind, before you start thinking about building any kind of investor presentation or penning any emails, it's an extremely valuable exercise first to develop your investment narrative script.

Your script is a short story that includes all the elements of your investment proposal that we covered in Step 1, with added colour and cadence to make it more engaging. It doesn't need to be complicated: indeed, the simpler your story, the more memorable it will be. You probably don't need more than a sentence or two, or perhaps a short paragraph, to describe each point in your investment proposal, which means you should be able to write out your story in no more than two or three sides of A4.

From a structural perspective, all good stories have a beginning, middle and end.

The beginning: draw the audience in

The start of your story is where you set the scene, agitate your listener and create drama and intrigue. The parts of your investment proposal on Vision, Problem, Opportunity and Market Landscape that we covered in Step 1 are all part of this scene setting.

Begin by giving them a flavour of what your business is about: this makes the investor want to know more by creating anticipation:

- First, introduce your company name and vision statement.
- Second, ask a question to get the investor thinking and/or help them feel your customers' pain point.

For example, when I'm telling the story of my business, Enter The Arena, I often start my narrative in one of the following ways:

> *Did you know that only 1 per cent of venture funding goes to women-led start-ups, despite the fact that they perform 63 per cent better for investors?*
>
> *Imagine for a moment what it feels like to be a female founder building a business in the menopause space: struggling to raise investment in a world where 95 per cent of venture partners*

are men who really don't get it and feel uncomfortable about the subject.

Have you ever felt that someone has made their mind up about your skills and capabilities before you've even walked through the door to meet them in person?

Capture your founder story

A great story has an inspiring protagonist: so if it's appropriate, put yourself and your connection to this problem at the centre of your story.

For a business in the early stages, a value-based founder story is important to help sell the vision, particularly before you have any significant proof-of-concept or traction in the market. Investors in early-stage businesses are investing primarily in you, the founder – they need to understand what's driving you, your passion and your connection to this business, because as you face the challenge of growing your company, it will be this passion that sees you through.

Your founder story also enables you to establish your credibility and build rapport with investors, which compels them to continue listening to you.

Think back to when you had the 'lightbulb' moment for creating your start-up:

- What was going on at the time? Set the stage, describe the scene.
- What was the problem you saw going on, who was experiencing it?
- How were other ways of solving the problem letting this person down?

- How was this negatively impacting your or their life?
- What did you discover about how many other people experienced this problem, so you could see the size of this opportunity?

Pulling these points together is a great way to build your early narrative.

The middle: reveal your business

The 'meat in the sandwich' of your story is where the action really takes place, and you draw your audience in further. You've already set the scene, now you can explain what your amazing business is doing to solve the problem you've identified:

- how you have the edge
- how you're making money
- who your customers are, and how you reach them
- who the team is that's executing on the plan
- just how far you've come.

Refer to Step 1 and the information you pulled together on your Solution, Competitive Advantage, Customers, Business Model, Route to Market, Team and Traction.

Keep it simple, just a sentence or short paragraph on each is all that's needed.

The end: where the story goes next

The final part of your story is where you:

- reveal the promise of even more action in the future
- excite the investor with where the business is going next
- say how you're going to create further growth and value.

This is where you'll cover 'The Promise', including your road map, results and exit plans (which we covered in Step 1).

Finally, the postscript: does your audience like the narrative, and do they want to be part of the next chapter? The end of your story is where you put forward your investment deal or ask, and hand back over to your audience to see if they would like to invest.

Once you've written out your story, read it back out loud to check it flows and makes sense. You might even want to record yourself reading it, re-listen or tell it to a trusted friend or advisor. You should be able to tell your story in around 5–10 minutes.

STORY: COMMUNICATING WITH EVERYDAY INVESTORS

Ashleigh Bishop, Bagboard

Bagboard is an advertising technology (AdTech) company that makes smart paper shopping bags and sells advertising space on them to conscious brands. It's a very clever solution and circular rewards scheme that makes shopping sustainable, which will no doubt have a huge impact on the number of plastic bags we use, as well as helping advertisers connect with consumers effectively.

Ashleigh founded Bagboard as one of three co-founders who had never raised or run a business before. They've since raised a total of around £3 million in funding, including a pre-launch 'friends and family' raise of £500,000, and a £600,000 round via crowdfunding in 2020.

But the investment journey wasn't easy. One of the biggest challenges Ashleigh faced was getting the pitch and the narrative right at every stage:

'We were fortunate through our network that we were able to fund the early days through friends and family. None of us had ever raised investment before, we'd never run our own business, and we tried to put together an investment pack by ourselves – the first one was about 100 pages!

We quickly learned this was not appropriate, and too much information. Everything you think is important about your business, halve it, halve it and halve it again, and get to the absolute nub of it. We needed support and guidance in doing that. One of the biggest challenges for any person trying to raise funds is to understand that what you think is crucial and important, versus what people need to hear, to understand the opportunity – there's quite a big gap between those two things.

Following our first funding round with angel investors, a corporate venturing arm and some grant funding in 2018, while we were still in pre-launch phase, we decided to raise further funds through crowdfunding in 2020. Bagboard is a complex concept to explain to the everyday crowdfunding investor when they can't even see the product in market, so understanding how to communicate to this new audience of investors was a real challenge.

We originally went out with our crowdfunding campaign for about a week, but quickly realised the original "rewards focus" of our narrative wasn't resonating with the audience. We had to completely revise our whole pitch to refocus the narrative around AdTech, which was a real challenge and a lot of sleepless nights – but you need to be OK with being a little bit reactive.

We subsequently saw the engagement we were looking for, so we could close the round.'

Build your pitch deck

A pitch deck is the communication tool you need to present your narrative to investors, and is the de facto standard in the start-up industry for raising investment. It's usually created using PowerPoint or a similar presentation tool, and generally around 15–20 pages or slides, sometimes a little longer.

This sounds like a simple thing to produce, but a pitch deck can be one of the hardest parts to nail when you're preparing for your fundraising campaign. It needs to be outstanding, because investors see hundreds of pitch decks every month – and they're incredibly efficient in evaluating the opportunity.

Investors spend on average only 3 minutes 18 seconds browsing your pitch deck to decide if you might make the cut. And guess what? No surprises: female founders come under way more scrutiny on their pitch decks; investors spend 44 per cent more time on the Business Model section of all-female decks than on all-male decks, 107 per cent more time on the Opportunity section, and 65 per cent more time on the Traction section.[1]

Knowing how important your pitch deck is can be a real blocker for some female founders, as we get caught up in perfectionism, working on version after version when it's more important to just get out there and speak with investors.

This procrastination usually belies the real underlying issue, as we've already discussed: a fear of failure in raising investment. This really is one of those occasions where the phrase 'Done is better than perfect' comes into play.

Be tough with yourself and set a firm deadline to get your pitch deck finished.

A few important things to note:

- There's no such thing as the perfect pitch deck – indeed, everyone you speak to has a different opinion on it.
- It's advisable to adapt your presentation for each investor meeting, to make sure it resonates with them.
- Expect to evolve your pitch deck as you speak to investors and get their feedback.

Your pitch deck is a tool to support you in your conversations with investors, not a crutch, something to hide behind or do the job of selling your investment proposition for you by itself.

When created and used correctly, it will help you:

- build rapport with your investor
- show how your business can provide investors with a great return on their investment, and feel good about backing you
- qualify the investor as someone you want to work with
- support you in closing commitment.

More than anything, your pitch deck's purpose is to help you tell a powerful investment story, and have investors biting their hands off to back you. The aim is to:

- engage your audience
- share and draw them into your passion and belief
- take them on a journey
- have a potential investor excited about what you could accomplish together.

Create your slides

Once you've nailed your investment narrative script, you're ready to build the suite of slides in your pitch deck to support that narrative, which you can then tweak and adapt for different investors and situations.

Different pitch decks for different purposes

Your presentation slides will be different, depending on how you intend to use them. There are four versions of the deck you may need: main, teaser, follow-up and presentation. Start by building your main deck, then you can alter the slides for the others as appropriate.

Main deck

This is your primary pitch deck, to be used in an investor meeting to help support your conversation. It's usually around 15–20 slides, and covers all the key areas investors need to know about.

Teaser deck

This can be sent to investors when you first reach out to them, to enable you to get a meeting. It's usually short, perhaps five to seven key slides, giving just enough information for the investor to see if this opportunity might be a fit for them, and be excited enough to want to discuss it with you in person.

Follow-up deck

This is sent following an investor meeting (if required), and may include more complex slides and appendices which can be read and absorbed by the investor in their own time.

Presentation deck

This is like an in-person deck, but designed to be more impactful to a larger audience: perhaps in a boardroom, or even at an event on stage. It might need to be abbreviated to meet a time allocation, which can be as short as 3–5 minutes.

The slides should use very little copy so they can be viewed from a distance, and to avoid the audience reading the slides instead of watching and listening to you.

Outline the structure and content of your pitch deck

Before you design beautiful looking slides, focus on getting the basic outline right.

1. Create a blank slide or page for each element of your investment proposal. Ultimately, you might need a couple of slides for some elements, but you can build that out later.
2. Add a title to each slide that conveys the key point you want to make, rather than one that simply says, 'Problem' or 'Solution'. That way, if all a potential investor does is flip through your slide headings, they'll be able to understand your whole narrative.
3. Add a few key bullet points on each slide that summarise what you want to say, and include any key facts and figures you want to mention.
4. If you have ideas at this stage about how you might visualise and illustrate your points in an engaging way, just make a note – don't get lost in trying to create the design.
5. Include a summary slide at the end, picking out five or six compelling reasons why someone might want to invest.
6. Outline any slides you might want to include as appendices for supplementary information, which don't need to be in your main story: consider further questions that investors might ask – for example, details on your operational set up, or a breakdown of your marketing plan.

Design your slides

With your structure and content laid out, it's time for the polish: you're ready to create beautifully designed slides to bring your investment story to life.

Your presentation must be professional. In the same way that your fundraising mindset is a mirror of your business (a concept we covered earlier in Chapter 4), your pitch deck must reflect how you want to be perceived – smart, well-presented, clear, dynamic, contemporary – whatever works for you and your brand.

Some design tips and hints to keep in mind:

- Keep copy bullet-pointed and succinct – avoid writing paragraphs of text, so your audience isn't caught up in reading your pitch, as opposed to listening to you.
- Use the principle of 'show, don't tell' to bring your story to life and help you communicate complex data simply – a picture tells a thousand words.
- Product screengrabs or even a short product demo video clip can work well when explaining your solution.
- Use photographs to show investors, for example, who your typical customer is, or help them picture the problem that customers are experiencing.
- Diagrams are great at conveying complex data quickly – especially useful when explaining operational processes, or how your marketing strategy hangs together.
- Competitor comparison tables or a matrix are helpful in quickly showing how you're positioned in the market.
- Use a chart or graph to show your revenue and profit growth plans, as your growth trajectory can be seen immediately.
- KPIs work well in a table, allowing the audience to quickly zone in on the relevant numbers.

Look online at presentation templates for inspiration and ideas, but take care not to replicate them: your narrative and brand are uniquely yours. As such, your pitch deck should be too.

Pitch deck design is an area where there is real value in getting expert support from someone with direct experience. The last thing you want is 'death by PowerPoint' and a pitch deck with naff fonts, poor design and full of clip art.

If design isn't your thing, don't try and botch it!

STORY: WATERLESS TOILETS

Virginia Gardiner, Loowatt

Virginia is the founder, CEO and inventor of Loowatt, a waterless toilet addressing the fact that 40 per cent of the world doesn't have a toilet, and the rest of us are using solutions that aren't sustainable.

Loowatt received initial investment via innovation grants, angels and then most recently, via crowdfunding: to date, it has raised a total of £7.5 million in funding, with more than 800 individual investors now supporting Loowatt's mission.

These selected slides from Virginia's pitch deck are great examples of how iconography, photography, illustrations, diagrams, bullet points and logos can be used to explain things clearly and bring a story to life (Figures 9–14).

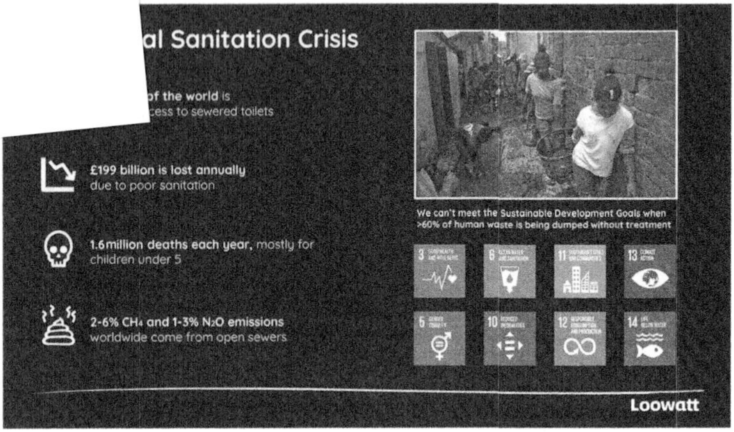

Figure 9: Problem slide

Figure 10: Market opportunity slide 1

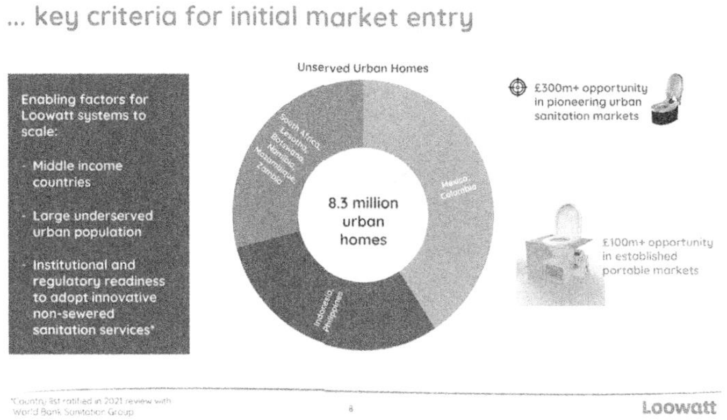

Figure 11: Market opportunity slide 2

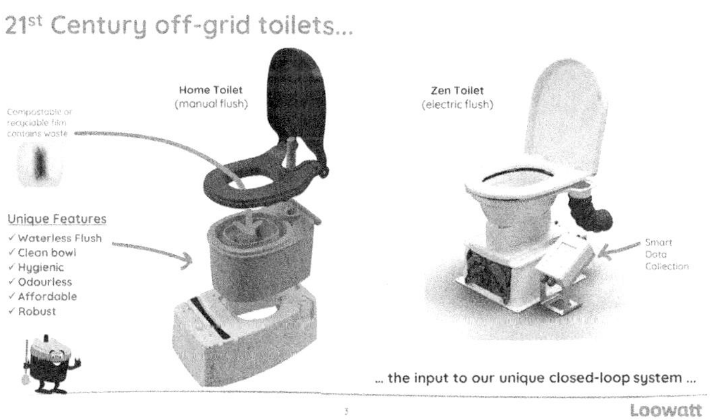

Figure 12: Solution slide 1

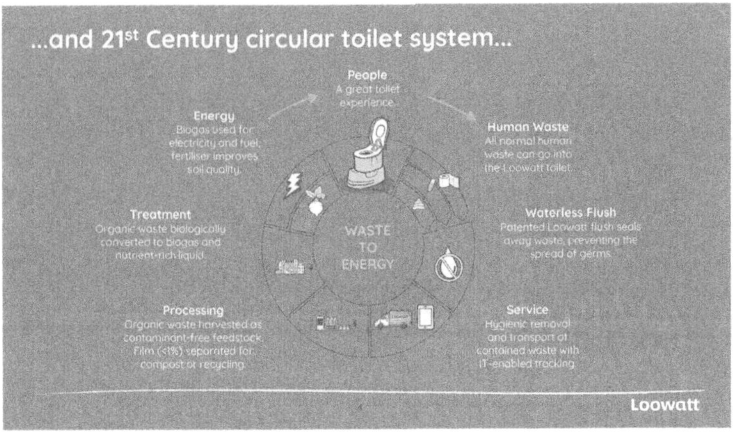

Figure 13: Solution slide 2

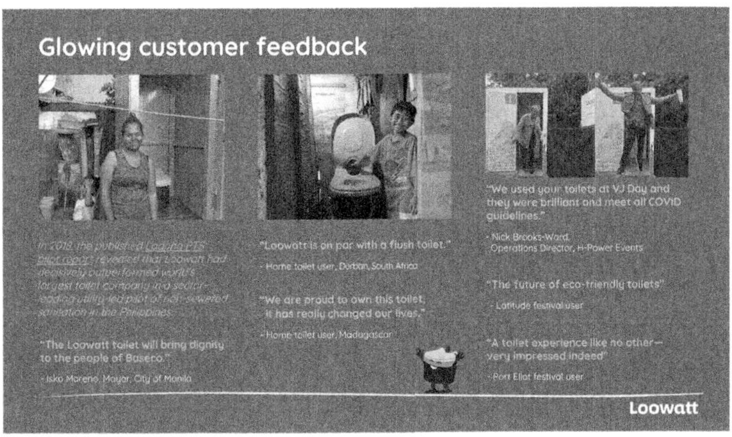

Figure 14: Traction slide

Create your pitch video

If you're crowdfunding, a pitch video is an essential asset required for your fundraising campaign; it can be a useful tool to communicate with other types of investors too. A video helps make an emotional connection, communicate all the essentials of your investment proposal and tell the story, even when you're not presenting live in person.

It doesn't have to cost a fortune to get a crowdfunding video made, but it does need to be high-quality. It's very possible to do the bulk of filming yourself with a smartphone, tripod and a decent light, and edit yourself using a movie editing tool.

Alternatively, consider using a small video production company: your budget will partly depend on how high you need your production values to be, which will be influenced by your brand, but you'll probably be looking at a few thousand pounds. Maximise your return on investment by reusing footage for other marketing purposes.

The ideal length of a crowdfunding video is 3–4 minutes, and it can be useful to have a much shorter edited version of around 30 seconds which can be used on social media channels.

Follow these preparation steps before filming your video:

1. write a script
2. get sign-off from the crowdfunding platform
3. create a storyboard.

Write your script

This will be a shorter, punchier version of the narrative you produced for your pitch deck. Practise and rehearse it as much as possible to ensure you can keep it within the time limit.

Get sign-off

Ensure your chosen crowdfunding platform conducts full due diligence on your script to fact check everything you're going to say. There's nothing worse than spending time and money on a great crowdfunding video, getting it fully produced and finished then submitting it to the platform, only for it to be rejected because you can't evidence something you've claimed in the script.

Create a storyboard

This is a plan that shows the video shots that go with the script. For each part of your story, think about how you could best show that visually.

For example:

- capture your customers experiencing the problem, and show how your solution solves it
- showcase video testimonials from customers and investors
- film your team at work
- consider where graphic overlays or animation might add value.

STORY: A GEM OF A VIDEO

Jenny Costa, Rubies in the Rubble

Jenny founded Rubies in the Rubble in 2011 after learning that one-third of food is wasted. Her vision was to produce 'conscious condiments' in a world where throwing away food has become the norm.

Starting the business initially as a passion project, creating small-batch chutneys and jams from surplus ingredients that otherwise would go to waste, she quickly went from selling at farmer's markets to scaling her business through supermarket distribution.

She raised investment from purpose-driven VCs, then had a successful crowdfunding campaign that was hugely lifted by their pitch video.

> *'We decided to try crowdfunding because we knew it would be fast... We had most of our pitch ready, so we just needed to create a video. We put a tight script together, filmed everything in our office with props that we made in-house by hand, which took a day, and then we had another day of editing.*
>
> *For me, the most important thing was having the tight script, and rehearsing and rehearsing the script so that it flowed well. I think words are so powerful, so make sure you use the right words that really convey what you're getting across. Then the filming becomes very quick and easy as well because you're flowing through it, and it's punchy and it keeps moving.*
>
> *We put some free music behind it, and away we went. The video for us was a way of showing a bit of personality about the brand and getting our story out. Then we went live with a target raise of £300,000... and within about 10 days, we hit £500,000.*
>
> *At the same time, I think just having that video – we started reaching out to people again, from VCs to professional investors. They suddenly got interested and got excited, and could see some momentum: a video just shows the personality of a brand. Suddenly, you're not just another chutney or a ketchup brand. The video really helped push that.*
>
> *We ended up closing our round, which included those large institutional investors, at £2.1 million.'*

Assess your external marketing

It's all well and good having a beautifully crafted pitch deck or a compelling video, but if the rest of your external communication doesn't match up, it's going to raise questions (and eyebrows) from potential investors.

The first thing an investor will do before having a conversation with you is look at your website, personal and business social media profiles, and any other external marketing communication they might come across.

First impressions really matter, so make sure the messaging and presentation is as good as it can be, and aligned with your pitch:

- Check any graphics and banners used online – to ensure your brand guidelines have been applied, and carry the correct tagline for the business.
- Make sure any copy describing your business is in line with the messaging in your investor pitch.
- Ensure your LinkedIn profile does you justice – that it represents you effectively as an outstanding entrepreneurial leader, with the right skills and experience to take your start-up to the next level.
- If you're comfortable going public on your fundraising campaign, create a page on your website to explain the opportunity, and set up a form to capture the details of interested investors. Link to your social media profiles to widen your communication reach.

Write your elevator pitch

Being able to describe yourself and your business in a single sentence is incredibly useful, as you never know when you might meet someone who could invest. You can really pack a punch with your elevator pitch, if you're clever!

Consider just how much powerful information is included in this example introduction, from a founder who has just met an angel investor in the lift on the way to an event:

> *'Hi, it's great to meet you! I'm a serial, successful entrepreneur building a market-leading cycle helmet business that's going to be worth £100 million in five years' time, because we're revolutionising the safety of millions of cyclists all over the world.'*

I'd certainly want to know more, wouldn't you? This short sentence tells the investor that this individual:

- has a good track record
- is ambitious
- is clear on their goals
- understands about building value
- has a specific timeline in mind
- is targeting a large global market
- is making real impact for their customers.

Consider how you might apply these principles to you and your business, and aim to include:

- your skills and experience
- a clear explanation of the business
- ambitious goals and timelines on building value

ɔpportunity

ɿaking a difference.

Prepare investor emails

There are many ways in which you can showcase your start-up to potential investors, but don't underestimate the power of the humble email, when well-crafted and used in the right way.

Emails to potential investors need to be well planned and thought out, just like the rest of your investor strategy. Often, those hundreds of emails that investors receive every week are epic essays, with every tiny conceivable detail about the founders' business and product, a bunch of attachments and no personal introduction.

An investor isn't going to read an email like that, even if it's come through a strong introduction – there simply aren't enough hours in the day.

One poorly executed email can turn an investor off you and your start-up forever – and if you try and tell your life story, or send too much information too soon, it's game over. Keep it short, and focus on what's in it for them.

Here are some top tips on how to craft email templates that cut through the noise, while respecting investors' time.

Title

Have a compelling title to your email that encourages them to open it. This is likely to be different, depending on whether you're sending it to your network of people who know you, or professional investors.

Be more creative with the subject line than the ty
business opportunity' or 'Seeking investment'.
going to cut it.

Your vision statement can be a good place to start: for example, I might introduce my business, Enter The Arena, with a title like:

'Making a real impact for female founders'

'Join us to close the gender funding gap'

– or more controversially:

'Are female founders a poor investment?'

Connect

Leave a space at the beginning of your email where you can personalise your opener: perhaps referring to the introducer who connected you (more on this in Chapter 8), or making it clear why you believe this person could be a good fit. It could be something you admire about their achievements, a report they've authored that influenced you, or an investment they've made that impressed you.

Build rapport, as flattery will get you a long way. (We'll be looking at this in more detail in Chapter 9.)

Business overview

Explain your business in one or two sentences maximum. It must be clear what you do, right from the outset.

Traction

Include two or three key indicators of your traction and success so far in the market. Also, you can include how much the company valuation has increased over the last few years, if appropriate. Confidently explaining your progression increases your agency and power.

Growth plans

Explain why you're raising investment, and what you expect to achieve over the next few years in terms of results and impact. This shows the potential for growth and your ambition.

Investment ask

Outline the kind of investment you're looking for, so they know what your ask is, and pre-qualify the type of investors you want on board. You want to effectively repel investors that won't be a fit and attract ones that might be, so you don't waste time. (We'll be looking at different types of investors in Chapter 9.)

Round progress

Indicate the timing of the round, and mention any progress you've already made in securing commitment from investors. This creates urgency and scarcity, and a bit of fear of missing out, which drives a lot of investors to act.

Call to action

Be clear about what you would like them to do next. If they're potentially interested in investing, suggest you have a call to discuss further, and ask when they would like to schedule that.

If it's not the right fit for them, ask who they know that might be interested. Or you might want to ask them for 'advice' as a slightly softer approach, which can be a highly effective way of getting a conversation started. Always have an ask.

Attachments

You may wish to include your introductory teaser deck with your initial email. Keep your main deck back for discussion with an investor in a meeting, where you'll be able to talk through the full opportunity in more detail. (We'll discuss investor meetings in detail in Chapter 9.)

Style and medium

Keep the tone of your email communications relaxed, confident and friendly: play it cool, so you don't come across as desperate. And one further point: it doesn't have to be an email – your communication could be a social media message, old-fashioned letter or phone call.

Once you have all your communication tools prepared – pitch deck, elevator pitch and email messages – you'll be ready to start making those all-important investor connections, as we move on to Step 4 in the fundraising process.

Action steps

1. Set yourself a hard deadline for getting your pitch deck done, so you don't procrastinate or get caught up trying to make it perfect.

2. Create your investment narrative script, which ideally should be no more than two to three sides of A4. Grab the audience's attention early, set the scene by weaving in your founder story, and build excitement as you reveal everything about your business and this exciting future ahead of you.

3. Check your narrative flows well by re-reading your script out loud, listening to a recording of it, and road testing it with a trusted friend or advisor.

4. Build the content and structure of your pitch deck based on your narrative script, focusing on headlines and bullet points of what you want to include. Remember, the slides are there to support what you're saying, so just highlight the key messages. Aim for no more than 15–20 slides. Include a summary

slide, and appendices with supplementary information that won't fit into your main deck.

5. Once your content and structure are ready, engage a professional designer to create a beautiful set of slides that communicate your message in a compelling way and reflect your brand effectively – that you feel proud to present to an investor.
6. Make sure your external marketing communications, including social media channels, website, brochures, etc. are aligned with the messaging and branding in your investment pitch – investors will be looking at these, when assessing your proposition.
7. Create a short, compelling elevator pitch to introduce yourself and your business in one or two sentences – you never know when you might meet someone who could be an investor.
8. If you're going to make a pitch video, approach production in the same structured way: script, storyboard, film. You don't need a huge budget but get creative, and be sure to get due diligence sign-off at script stage if you're crowdfunding.
9. Prepare a template email you can use to connect with potential investors.

8
Step 4: Connection

The first three steps we've covered are all about preparing your fundraising assets. Now in Step 4 comes the exciting (or perhaps daunting!) phase where you start actively talking with investors.

Who are these investors, where do you find them – and how do you connect effectively with them?

First, it's important to understand more about the different types of investors, and which ones might be a good fit for you. Then, we'll look at how to reach out to them and make a powerful connection.

Factors influencing the investors you seek

The type of investors you look for usually depends on several factors.

Your raise amount

How much money do you need to raise, both now and in the future?

Different types of investors will invest varying amounts of money, which can be as little as £10 or as much as several million. Some may be able to invest in several rounds on your journey, while others won't – so for example, there is little point speaking to 'big ticket' investors if you're raising your first seed round of £150,000.

Your stage of business

How far along the growth journey is your company?

As your business gathers momentum, the investment opportunity carries lower risk, and will attract different types of investors whose risk appetite can vary quite considerably.

Some will be comfortable coming in while you're at idea stage, while others will want to see that your business has already launched; some get excited getting on board where you're in the early stages of proving product-to-market fit, while many prefer to wait until you're you've figured out the mechanics of your business, and now need money to scale (Figure 15).

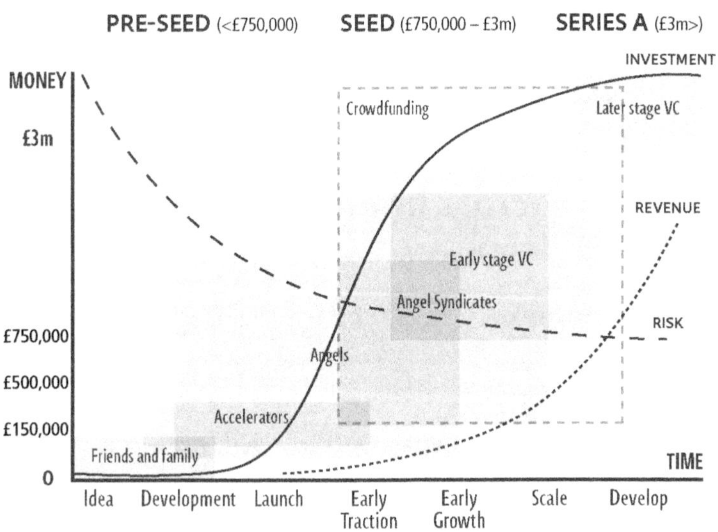

Figure 15: Different investors at different stages

Map the type of investor you might approach to the amount of money you're looking to raise, and your stage of business. If it's sub-£150,000 and you're very early on, consider friends and family, accelerators or angel investment.

If you're raising more and the business is getting more traction, then angel syndicates and family offices can be an option. If you're looking to raise more than £250,000 and are a little more established, then you could be in early-stage VC territory. Crowdfunding can work for all raise amounts, and you can invite all types of investors to participate in this.

Your growth ambitions

How big and fast can (and do) you want to grow your business?

Some investors look to back a company which could become a 'unicorn' (i.e. can achieve a valuation of at least $1 billion [£800 million]), giving them a fast and huge return on their investment while accepting the higher risk that might come with that. Others are looking for a longer-term, less risky play, and accept more modest potential returns, backing businesses that take more time to grow: this is called 'patient capital'.

You'll need to find the right fit for you, both in terms of speed and size of the opportunity for growth.

Your type of business and industry sector

Many investors only back specific types of companies, which might be because they have direct experience in that area, have determined this is a sector they want to back due to market trends, or perhaps to balance out their portfolio.

For example, if you're building an e-commerce business, finding investors that get this space is going to be important; if you're a fashion brand, there's little point in speaking with investment funds that only put money into Software as a Service (SaaS) businesses.

The support you're looking for

How closely do you want your investors to be involved in helping you grow the business?

Some investors like to roll up their sleeves and get stuck in, or might require a board seat. Others prefer to stay at arm's length if you keep them informed on progress from time to time. Get clear on any specific skills and experience you want investors to bring, and the type of working relationship you envisage with them.

The quality of your early investment rounds is important: having reputable investors on board not only helps you in growing your business, but also improves your chances of securing further funding from other people or institutions in future.

Let's explore the different types of investors, their typical profiles and what they tend to look for when it comes to backing start-up companies.

Types of investor

Friends and family

'Friends and family' goes much wider than the literal definition, because it includes all the people in your personal network. This is a typical first source of equity funding for many founders, especially for a raise of up to £150,000, with the average friends and family round being £70,000.[1]

When you're in the early stages of building your business, most professional investors won't be interested because they see too much risk; whereas those who know you more intimately are more likely to have confidence that you have what it takes to make your business idea work. They've seen how dedicated you are, have watched you working hard over the years, and know you have the smarts to give it your best shot. Your own network is often the best place to start activating your fund-raising campaign.

You might only expect to get reasonably small amounts from a friends and family investor – likely in the range of a few thousand to a few tens of thousands – although of course, it depends on the amount of funds an individual has available and is prepared to risk. As these people don't often have a great deal of experience (if any) in investing in start-ups, it's important they understand the risks involved before they commit.

Many founders assume that the people they know don't have money to invest. But it can be a mistake to draw those conclusions, as you may not really know what their financial situation is – and remember, even if they're unable to invest, they may know someone who can.

You might also feel uncomfortable asking people you know to 'give you money'. But there is an exchange of value here: you're offering them an opportunity to own a share of your business and go on the venture journey with you – with the express intention of making a return on their investment.

Any uncomfortable feelings you have around offering this to people can be a sign that you might need to re-examine your investment proposal, and probably also your mindset, to see what's knocking your confidence. Because if your belief is rock-solid, why wouldn't you give them the chance to come on board? They can only say 'No'.

As to whether friends and family investors want involvement in your business or have expertise to offer you, very much depends on the individual and what you're comfortable with in terms of mixing business with personal. But generally, friends and family are happy to invest their money and let you get on with it – if you keep them posted on how things are going.

STORY: STARTING WITH PEOPLE YOU KNOW

Jessica and Louella Alderson, So Syncd

Sisters Jess and Lou have tapped a fresh niche in the online dating market, using personality-type profiling for a perfect match, launching So Syncd in January 2020.

They've taken their market by storm, and in a short time managed to raise more than £700,000 in investment. Before setting up the business, Jess worked as an equity research analyst at Morgan Stanley, and Lou was one of the first employees at Empiric Student Property, where she helped to scale the company from a valuation of £80 million to more than £1 billion.

With the goal of building a marketable product as quickly as possible while they were still holding down full-time jobs, Jess and Lou started with a friends-and-family round. Here's what Jess had to say about how it went:

> *'Our own savings and salaries got us to launching the MVP [Minimum Viable Product]. We didn't really have much of a marketing budget, but despite that we grew a lot quicker than we expected, and a lot quicker than we'd forecast in our business plan. Then we were like, "Right. This is now time for a proper product", but we definitely didn't have time to actually build a proper product.*
>
> *So we raised £100,000 though friends and family, that essentially enabled us to rebuild the app and quite a bit more. That round*

was primarily through people that we knew; it was just asking friends of friends and stuff like that. It was relatively quick.

I haven't found it very comfortable to ask people I know. I imagine it's the kind of thing that probably a man would find a bit easier to do than a woman would? There are some friends I didn't ever mention it to, because I didn't think they would have invested. But they've all come to me now and said, "I would've invested," and I say back, "I didn't ask you because I thought it would be a bit awkward."

I regret this now. It's difficult when you're quite close to someone, you don't want to put them in a difficult position, but I think you just have to ask. They can just say "No" and it's fine.

Also, it doesn't need to be ridiculous amounts. Small amounts do add up. If you get smaller amounts from, say five, 10 people, then that adds up quickly.

Eventually we had just over 20 investors in our friends and family round. I think it's just being bold and asking.'

Start-up accelerators

There are a great many, and increasing number of, accelerator programmes available to founders (currently more than 7,000 worldwide,[2] with 200 in both the UK and USA respectively),[3] to support them through the challenges of building their start-up with training and mentoring.

Some of these accelerators provide investment either on acceptance into the programme, or at a pivotal point when you've passed certain criteria. Most focus on specific sectors, with technology and social impact being the most popular,[4] although some have quite broad selection criteria. Most are supported by corporate sponsors or non-profit organisations.

There are a number that focus exclusively on female founders (you'll find some of the more well-known ones in the Further Resources).

Accelerator programmes usually run over several weeks or months and are often cohort-based. There is tough competition to get on to most programmes, especially the best known and respected ones, such as Seedcamp, Startupbootcamp and Techstars – but they can really raise your profile in the investment ecosystem, and segue you into reaching investors for your next fundraising round if you need it, as well as providing many other benefits.

Where provided, the amount of funding tends to be quite small (less than £30,000), although some accelerators invest as much as £100,000; typically, the accelerator takes 5–10 per cent of equity in return. They tend to come in at an early stage where your business is still very high-risk, which is why they expect a very modest valuation.

It's expensive, but there is great value in being part of a programme, if you find the right fit for you. Companies that attend accelerators raise 44 per cent more money, and achieve 75 per cent higher valuations, than those that don't.[5]

If you're keen on getting funding via an accelerator, you can find lists online via a quick Internet search (although I have yet to find one that is complete or up-to-date). Working out which ones might be a fit for you is a matter of sifting through and doing your research, or working with a trusted advisor to help guide you.

STORY: ACCELERATING SOCIAL PLANS

Louise Doherty, Yoller

In 2016, fed up with sorting out all the social plans for her group, Louise created Yoller, the app that helps people organise real-world get-togethers more easily through an artificial intelligence social planning platform – since featured by Apple and Google as one of the best apps for socialising in more than 140 countries.

To date, Louise has raised £1 million in equity funding for her business from corporate investors, angel syndicates and through crowdfunding. But it was being accepted onto the Techstars business accelerator in the early days that really helped springboard her success.

> *'I took a brilliant consulting gig for a couple of years, and put almost every penny I made into saving to make Yoller happen. I realised, once I was underway with prototyping the product, that raising investment at this early stage might be tricky, and that maybe an easier thing to do would be go straight to revenue.*
>
> *We got our first contract before the product was built. That early traction and that initial customer was a proof point that meant we could go to other sources of funding.*
>
> *'My first employer became our first investor, and at around the same time we got into Techstars, the business accelerator in New York. Those two things happening gave us a good grounding, some clear runway and allowed us to hire a team, and it spiralled from there.*
>
> *The place on the programme came with funding that was broken out into two different vehicles: part loan, part equity. Suddenly we're not just one of these thousands of early-stage companies, we've been elevated to this special status of being a Techstars*

company, which was important in the USA because it's a brand of credibility that translates in a way some of our other achievements didn't.

Obviously just getting into Techstars doesn't mean you're an instant overnight success – it's still a lot of hard work – but it makes you stand out, and that really helped us early on.

Today there are many accelerators to choose from, with roughly the same money on offer but totally different value propositions: will they grow your network, build your customer base, help you find a co-founder or a team, teach you how to scale or develop you as a person into a leader?

There is no "best accelerator", but there might be a best one for you, based on the delta between your unique DNA and your big vision.'

Angel investors

These are private individuals, also known as High Net Worth Individuals (HNWI), who invest their own money in start-ups. Sometimes this is their sole profession, more often they're people who work in high-paid jobs with a lot of disposable net income, or successful entrepreneurs who want to put some of their money back into venture.

The typical profile of an angel investor is white, male, aged 50+. At the time of writing, only around 15–18 per cent of angel investors are women.[6]

Angel investors usually invest somewhere between £10,000 and £50,000 per deal, with a median initial investment of £25,000.[7] Often, they're strongly motivated to invest in a business where they feel personally connected with the mission, or have relevant expertise or knowledge. As such, it's worth noting that female angel investors are much more likely to invest in female founders.

Angel investors may offer their skills, experience and an extensive contacts book to support you as well as funding, which can be a very positive thing; however, some angels can be quite meddlesome. Sometimes they come in early, at idea stage, as well as when your business is more established.

If you're seeking angel investment, the best bet is to find people who understand your industry or sector, as they'll be more likely to get what you do quickly and see the opportunity ahead:

- **Who are the successful entrepreneurs in your industry?** They may have money to invest, as entrepreneurs love to give back – they remember how important it was to get that leg up and the difference that investment made for them. Successful entrepreneurs also tend to have the right risk profile for investing in venture, and are likely to know professional investors in your space.
- **Who are the other influential people in your industry?** Research senior leaders in big corporates or chairs of professional bodies, as these are all people who may have money to invest, or who could lead you to others who can.
- **Who has funded other companies in your sector?** Look on crowdfunding platforms (we'll be looking at these later in this chapter), CrunchBase.com, search online for press releases, and network with your peers to see which angel investors have backed them.

STORY: ADVISORS AS INVESTORS

Merilee Karr, UnderTheDoormat

Merilee is the CEO and Founder of UnderTheDoormat: an award-winning, luxury short-term rental company, enabling modern travellers to enjoy the comfort of a home with the professional service of a hotel.

Merilee started UnderTheDoormat in 2014 after 13 years working in a big corporate. Since launch, she has raised a total of around £2.5 million in equity finance to grow the business through several different fundraising rounds, primarily angels and family offices.

But it was her strategy of bringing on board advisors early on, who also invested, that really helped her get the company off the ground.

> *'Understanding which capital you want to go for is a strategic decision every entrepreneur should take very early on in your journey, because being purposeful about that is really important.*
>
> *At the beginning, I funded the business myself with a £20,000 personal loan into the company. Then very quickly, I had a board of advisors that I put together as I launched the business. I look back and that was probably one of the best decisions I made: I had experts – technology, finance, legal, marketing, etc. – and they formalised their role with the company as a board of advisors, because they were passionate about the idea, and wanted to be involved in making it happen.*
>
> *I offered them the opportunity to buy shares in the business very early on. That was my first friends and family round, and I raised about £100,000 at that point in time. We took the approach of a small amount early on to preserve ownership, and it was only three years into the business before we then*

went on to do our first seed round, and brought on industry and strategic angel investors, as well as a small top-up on crowdfunding for the PR value.

Most of our angel investors are people who come from the hospitality or property industry.'

Angel syndicates

An angel syndicate or network is where private groups of individuals come together to make investments: around 79 per cent of angel investment takes place in this way.[8]

Often, one of the more experienced angels will lead on a deal, which means they take on the responsibility of recommending the investment to others and undertaking due diligence, then the others in the group choose whether they want to invest. A syndicate might make that investment as one entity, with their money pooled through a fund, or the angels in the group might each invest individually in the business.

Syndicates are very active in seed funding, preferring to get involved with early-stage businesses where there is potential for greater returns and attractive tax breaks. Typically, the funding amounts available are between £100,000 and £2 million. Some syndicates invest across all sectors and business types, while others have a more specific focus, such as technology or sustainability, or invest only in a particular geographical region.

Usually, they expect your business to have some proof of product-to-market fit.

Female-focused investors

There are an increasing number of angel networks and funds focusing specifically on under-represented founders, with some investing in women-led start-ups, recognising this untapped potential in the market.

Although the sums available are still modest, it is encouraging (you'll find these referenced in the Further Resources).

Family offices

Family offices are private professional firms that actively manage the wealth of Ultra High Net Worth (UHNWI) individuals or families, and are a rapidly growing source of direct investment for start-ups.

On average, A single-family office manages assets of around £590 million. If they manage multiple families (around 20), assets average around £1.1 billion.[9] Typically, a family office allocates 12 per cent of these funds to venture investments, with 55 per cent of those being made directly into the start-up, and 45 per cent via VC funds.[10]

The amount that family offices have invested in European start-ups has increased fivefold[11] in recent years, as the returns available from other assets have become less attractive compared with those in tech start-ups. Also, as more wealthy entrepreneurs have been created, they choose to invest back into venture. There has been a large increase in money coming from the newly-wealthy Asian region, too.

Family offices are patient investors that are prepared to work with start-ups over a long period before getting returns, as they answer only to themselves rather than having to meet obligations to shareholders or funds. They can make decisions on investments relatively quickly, and add real strategic value with their skills, experience and connections.

Typically, these investors aren't tied to a particular investment mandate; instead, they have personal interests, areas of expertise and philosophies on the start-up criteria they look for. Do bear in mind that if there is a change in management or the next generation of family take over, their objectives can change quickly. With a newer generation of family becoming involved, they can become increasingly keen on making an impact as part of their legacy, focusing on sustainable or ethical businesses; many are specifically interested in backing female-led start-ups.

Family offices are notoriously private and confidential – you rarely read about them in the press, and they might not even have a website – so it can be difficult to learn about and connect with them. Finding entrepreneurs who've been uber-successful in your space, who might now have their own family office to manage their wealth, is one strategy; another is asking professional services providers including lawyers, wealth managers and accountants for contacts.

Family offices often co-invest alongside other investors or source opportunities via leading accelerators, so this is another way of reaching them.

STORY: THE STRATEGIC VALUE OF INVESTORS

Joyce and Raissa de Haas, Double Dutch

Twin sisters Joyce and Raissa, co-founders of the premium tonic and mixers brand Double Dutch, moved to London aged just 21 to begin their entrepreneurial journey with a Master's degree at University College London (UCL) in Technology Entrepreneurship, where they came up with the idea for the business.

Six years on, Double Dutch was already selling more than a million bottles every month to 26 countries across the world, and had completed three funding rounds, including backing from their dream investors, the Heineken family.

> *'During our Master's, we devoted our year to writing down a new business plan. The whole gin hype had really started, but the choice of mixers was limited and there wasn't really anything exciting on the market. On graduation we won an award for best dissertation of the year, and UCL gave us grant money to execute our business plan.*
>
> *Then we used a little bit of our own money that we saved during university from student jobs, before we decided we needed to raise our first investment round, which we secured from a few angel investors whom we found via networking on LinkedIn.*
>
> *For our second round we decided to go again with new angel investors, as we wanted to get people that had a network behind them that could help us with distribution and sales and who could also help with strategy and long-term vision and execution, and share their experience. Lots of them were customers of ours that either owned pubs or hotels, or were CEOs of bigger retail companies we already knew.*
>
> *One of our investors on that round introduced us to the Heineken family. From our perspective, if there's one family in the world that we could choose to be an investor or a shareholder in Double Dutch, it would always have been Heineken – on a cultural level with Dutch heritage, their family business, everything.*
>
> *I think we were super, super, super lucky – it's amazing to have them on board.'*

Venture capital

VCs are institutional investors who manage other people's money (family offices, pension funds, HNWIs, etc.), which they secure, put into a fund (or several funds) and then invest into start-ups.

Early-stage VCs come in at the pre-seed or seed phase of investment, for round sizes that are usually a minimum of around £250,000 up to £2–3 million; and as we've seen previously, in the UK they often only invest in businesses that qualify for the EIS tax scheme. Later stage VCs invest in businesses where product-to-market fit is proved, route to market is established, a strong management team is in place, and the business is truly ready to scale, on a Series A round where investments are more than £2–3 million.

VCs are run on a 'partner' model, and tend to be very male-dominated. The latest data available show that only 13 per cent of decision-makers (partners or equivalent) in VC are women, while 48 per cent of investment teams have no women at all.[12]

A typical VC gets 1,000 approaches from start-ups each year, meets with around 10 per cent of them, and only invests in 1 per cent of them, so it's an extremely competitive environment for entrepreneurs. Most VCs are looking for unicorns, and most often for technology businesses which require less capital to scale – although every fund has its own investment criteria which is usually published on the VC's website.

VCs know from experience that nine out of 10 businesses they back will flatline or fail – which puts huge pressure on the founder to scale fast, or the VC will quickly drop them. It's do or die. On the plus side, when it's all going well, a VC is often able to follow on their money to support you (i.e. put more money in on a future investment round), as you scale further and need more cash – you can benefit from their experience in growing other great start-ups, as well as being a part of their portfolio.

Be aware, you'll usually need to cover the VC's legal fees on your deal transaction, and many VCs also charge start-ups an ongoing management fee of up to a few thousand pounds per month post-investment.

(There are some useful sources and links to institutional investors that specifically focus on funding female founders in the Further Resources.)

STORY: THE VALUE OF A VC

Jennifer Lam, Stitch & Story

Jennifer, who co-founded the digital crafts brand that's inspiring a new generation of knitting hobbyists, has successfully turned a kitchen start-up into a global business, fuelling growth with venture finance. After growing the business organically for the first few years, Jennifer raised first from angels, then via a venture capital firm.

> *'At the beginning I didn't know where I was heading. I just had this passion, I was young and full of energy, I had this "why" and I wanted to go and solve something. We went to market stalls, trade shows, workshops, bootstrapped our business and did everything we could on our small budget of £12,000, which we invested ourselves.*
>
> *But then hit a wall, as there was so much demand we couldn't handle it. That kicked our decision to look for outside investment, to really scale the business to its full potential. We first raised through a few angels, £125,000, and moved our business from our homes and grew the team. Then we were growing at*

3x year-on-year, there was so much demand – and for a start-up, cash flow is everything – so I knew I needed a further raise.

I must have spoken to about 20 venture capital firms, looking for investors that understood our vision, passion and the time frame, and the one we went with really got it. Knowing they provide an enormous amount of help, and are there to support the founders in any way was powerful for me – because I wanted to still be in the driving seat, I didn't want someone else to dictate where I should go. They'd also funded a lot of female-founded companies, so I felt like they checked that box as well.

We closed the first round of £1 million with them in November 2019, then a few months later Covid hit, and suddenly our sales were growing 800 per cent during the first lockdown. I spoke to our investor and said, "I need further investment, because I need to scale the team even bigger than I had planned because of the growth."

I saw the trend of well-being, mindfulness and creativity, a macro trend that is going to stay forever because the pandemic has changed the way consumers behave. I had a really clear direction of where I wanted to take us next, and our investor helped with more funding where the critical areas of growth was needed.'

Corporate investors

Strategic investment from a big corporate investor might be an option for you, depending on where you are on your growth journey. As well as the large tech players like Google and Microsoft, companies in many other vertical niches such as Fast-Moving Consumer Goods (FMCG), media, finance and healthcare now have funds to invest in start-ups which are innovating in their industry.

Strategic investors can help you with product development, partnerships, technology and so on – but ultimately, they might only be investing in you as a potential future acquisition. This may not align with what you or your other investors want, can limit your exit valuation or even block your potential exit, so this needs very careful thought – particularly in the early days before you've fully established yourself as a successful, independent company.

Crowdfunding

Equity-based crowdfunding enables you to source investment from 'the crowd'. This means anyone and everyone that self-identifies as being HNWI, 'sophisticated' (i.e. knows what they're doing) or will invest less than 10 per cent of their net assets, can put money into a start-up that is promoted on a crowdfunding platform.

Investors can put in as little as £10 each, depending on the platform rules, so you can end up with hundreds or even thousands of investors on a fundraising round, depending on how much you're raising. The information on a crowdfunding website is in the public domain, so you need to be comfortable with that.

Crowdfunding is best suited to those businesses that are already getting good traction, are easily understood by 'everyday investors', and have a strong network or customer base from which to secure investment.

More women-led start-ups raise through crowdfunding than other routes, with 24 per cent of crowdfunding deals going to female founders. Female founders tend to do well with a 75 per cent success rate, compared with a 55 per cent success rate for male-led start-ups raising this way.[13]

Crowdfunding investors are arms-length, unless you invite them to be more closely involved in your business. But the value of having hundreds of committed investors can be significant in building a tribe of brand ambassadors to help you raise awareness of your business in the market. Most professional investors keep a close eye on the leading crowdfunding platforms, so by raising money via this route, you also raise your profile with the wider investment ecosystem.

Friends and family, angel investors, angel syndicates and VCs can all participate in crowdfunding rounds, so it can be a great way to bring together disparate funding sources in an efficient way. Deal sizes have been getting increasingly large on crowdfunding platforms over the last few years, with some mega-deals of £5–10 million now taking place.

With crowdfunding, you don't get any of the money you need unless you hit your fundraising target, so it's important to set the minimum raise amount appropriately. To be successful, it's critical to have at least one-third of your fundraising target committed from investors in advance, if not more. This advanced commitment can be from professional or institutional investors, or from your own 'tribe' – so it's important to put in the legwork in advance, as the crowdfunding platform itself won't bring in those investors for you. Think of crowdfunding as topping up funding you've already secured, rather than being a sole source of investment.

Crowdfunding platforms usually allow you to list your business for 30–60 days, so a fundraise can happen quite fast. This is useful to stop a campaign dragging on, but it can bring an incredible amount of pressure to bear on you as a founder.

Crowdfunding platforms look after the technical and legal processes of getting the money in and closing your round, and can support and advise you throughout your campaign. Their fees vary, but you'll be looking at around 6–7 per cent of the amount you raise, plus a completion fee of approximately 1 per cent – plus you also may need to cover payment processing fees, as your crowdfunding investors will be using debit or credit cards for their transactions. (Some of the more well-known platforms are listed in the Further Resources.)

STORY: CONFIDENCE OF THE CROWD

Claire Ransom, Lazy Flora

Claire is the founder and CEO of Lazy Flora, an online plant store that makes gardening and plant ownership fun and hassle-free.

She launched in 2017 and self-funded over two years, rapidly growing her customer base. At that point, it was time to raise pre-seed equity investment, which she did via crowdfunding, for a total of £85,000.

> *'It's always been my ambition that the business will be big: I want it to be a new type of online garden centre that makes shopping and browsing for plants fun and approachable, rather than overwhelming and intimidating.*
>
> *I started Lazy Flora from my parents' house and did literally everything myself: packing boxes, sourcing plants, graphic design, website build, copy and marketing. It was bootstrapped for a long time with a tiny budget, with some savings from my job in publishing. By the second half of 2018, we had great month-on-month revenue and subscriber growth figures, and I knew I needed to raise some money if I really wanted to take it to the place that I knew it could get to – so I decided to crowdfund.*

It took a couple of months' preparation to get the campaign live, and then it ran for nearly two months. It was hard work and very intensive from start to finish, as I was building a network and investor base from absolutely zero.

Tapping into our existing customer base was effective. We didn't have a huge number of customers but they were very dedicated and engaged, and they were some of our earliest investors and honestly just made my heart burst.

Inside tip: when we were included in the crowdfunding platform's weekly newsletter to investors, we would get an influx of investment from people who didn't know the business, and who had never come across Lazy Flora before.

Our crowdfund gave me so much confidence in the business, because hundreds of crowdfunding investors saw the potential and results so far, which was just so amazing.'

To conclude this section, you may find it helpful to know how other founders assess the value of investors, as you consider which route to go yourself.

The top five criteria that founders use are, in order of priority:

1. good relationship and cultural fit
2. terms of the deal
3. individual partner expertise
4. good character
5. ability to fund the company over the long term.[14]

As you plan which route to go yourself, consider which criteria will be most important to you.

Plan your investor campaign

Whether you're looking to attract friends and family, angel investors, family offices, VC firms, crowdfunding or a mix of all of these, I recommend the same three-step approach: attract, qualify, close. Running your investment campaign effectively is about being laser-focused rather than scattergun.

There are three basic steps to follow:

1. **Build your target list.** This is an ongoing activity: you'll be adding to that list as you go, as people introduce you to others who might be a good fit. Start with your existing network, then move on to building this out to people you don't yet know.

2. **Reach out to investors in the right way.** Use your email message templates as a basis to connect with investors, with the aim of securing meetings with those who might be a good fit.

3. **Run your campaign like a military operation.** If you want to get your fundraising done fast and efficiently, you'll need to put your outreach activity right at the top of your to-do list every day.

Build your target list

As previously mentioned, your network is the best place to start, as these are the people that know, trust and like you. Plus you'll already have their details, usually in one or all the following places:

- personal address book
- existing LinkedIn connections

- customer database
- social media followers.

You'll be able to connect with these people over direct email, LinkedIn messaging, your customer relationship management (CRM), email marketing system, via social media through posts or direct messages.

You don't necessarily need to bring all these contacts into one single list, but it will be helpful for you to note:

- the outreach activity you make
- how many people you have reached
- the response rate.

As you get people interested, you may then wish to put those 'hot' leads into a single spreadsheet, so you can track your sales pipeline (we'll touch on how to manage your campaign later in this chapter).

STORY: AN INVESTED COMMUNITY

Emma Sayle, Killing Kittens

In 2005, Emma saw an opportunity to change the male-dominated adult industry, to make space for women to safely explore their sexuality. Emma is now at the helm of a global movement for female sexual empowerment.

This move, a necessity to develop the digital arm of the brand, was perfect – with the 'MeToo' movement in the zeitgeist and the rapid rise in the sex-tech sector. Emma secured her first investment round of £600,000 in 2018, much of which came from within the Killing Kittens (KK) community of more than 100,000 members at that time.

'I didn't want a raise that involved having City boys with lots of money investing, going round saying, "I own a sex business" type thing. It wasn't sitting comfortably, and with 120,000 members, it's always been about community. I'd rather have 400 people owning a small part of the business and putting in a tenner, and really being brand ambassadors. That's why we chose to crowdfund.

It was really humbling, because we had an overwhelming response from members – both women and men – many couples wanting to invest and wanting to get involved, and loads saying that we'd changed their lives and changed their relationships, or they owed us their marriage.

For the first time ever, we got a lot of feedback from members on the impact that being part of KK had on people. It was a real emotional investment for a lot of people. They got it because they'd lived and breathed KK for a decade, and could see the expansion themselves.

You can't make that up – it's just there, black and white on paper.

Sixty per cent of our funding came from those people who we already knew. To me, you've got to listen to your gut on the best route to go, when it comes to reaching out to investors. In my gut I was not feeling comfortable with going to the City with my pitch. Listen to your gut.'

Building out your network beyond those people you already know is an activity you should always be doing as a founder of a high-growth start-up, but never more so than when you're preparing for or raising investment.

Get introductions

Traditionally, investors have sourced their pipeline of potential founders to invest in from their network. This has been a very successful strategy for them, because they:

- are in the ecosystem
- are present at start-up events, every week
- know other leading angels or VC firms well, often co-investing alongside them
- have a wide network

– which means they get to meet entrepreneurs all the time.

The truth is, you're 13 times more likely to be invested in if you get a warm introduction through their existing network.[15]

However, if investors are mostly older, white guys, and their network tends to be made up of people who are like them, this attracts entrepreneurs that are also like them – which makes it challenging for female founders to infiltrate. The more progressive investors, who want to address inequalities in diversity, are looking at new ways to source deal flow and reach out to under-represented founder groups. They're more likely to have a well thought-through application process on their website which aims to strip out bias, but this is not always the case.

Use your existing network to help you build out your network further and reach those ideal investors you're looking for. LinkedIn is a useful social media tool to help build relationships with existing contacts and expand your network from there. Don't be afraid to ask directly for connections to new people you want to reach, because once you start those conversations

– and if you do it well – you'll find they'll introduce you to even more people, and it will roll from there.

It's the 'Six Degrees of Separation' effect: you're never more than six connections away from someone else in the world, and on LinkedIn that person is usually just one or maybe two connections away. Asking for an introduction is just a question of being brave, putting yourself out there and framing it in the right way.

STORY: CONNECTING THE DOTS

Pip Jamieson, The Dots

In 2009, Pip co-founded her first business in Australia called The Loop, a platform to help people in the creative industries network and find jobs.

After selling her share of the business, Pip returned to London and decided to start all over again by building a UK creative industries network called The Dots. Pip has raised £5.5 million in investment finance in the last few years with two major funding rounds, and the platform has more than half a million members.

Pip had no professional investors in her existing network in London, so started a serious round of networking, going for coffee with anyone who might be able to help. While there were lots of 'No's, Pip secured a cornerstone investor, which led to herding in the rest of them successfully and raising £1.5 million in the first round.

> *'I had zero network here in the UK. I couldn't be as strategic as I'd loved to have been. It was very much like, "Who do I know who can connect me with someone else?" Because I didn't have any network here, because I really didn't know any other founders*

here, it was just a lot of who would just take the meetings – and so those early days were taking any meeting I could.

And from there, basically, selling the vision, getting them excited about it, and then at the end of it making sure you have an ask, which is, "Do you know anyone that's an investor, or know anyone that you think would be interested?"

It was just a lot of graft. I would literally find anyone I knew that was in tech, and try and build out that way. My lucky break to my first round of investment came when a girl in my co-working space introduced me to a very high-profile entrepreneur and investor, and then he introduced me to an angel syndicate. Another investor came through one of my clients, whose daughter was in school with his children.

It's just insane how you have to connect the dots when you don't have that existing network.'

Professional introducers

Should you use a professional introducer to connect you with investors? At an early stage, investors want to meet you, the founder, rather than someone else pitching your business on your behalf.

Introducers work on a fee basis, so usually they only get paid when they bring you investment from their network: this 5 per cent fee can be a lot of money to pay out, just for someone introducing you. Bear in mind that their primary relationship is with their network of investors, and because they get paid a percentage of the investment amount, they don't necessarily care about the quality of the deal that is done – for example, valuation, deal terms, long-term viability, etc.

Pitch events and competitions

Pitch events can be an effective way to build out your network while also getting live experience presenting your business. They can be nerve-racking, but worth braving to strengthen your pitching skills, get useful feedback through the questions that investors ask, plus exposure to investors and other influencers in the start-up ecosystem.

Choose wisely which ones you apply for, as pitch events can be a real drain on time and resources.

STORY: DISCOVERING YOUR SPRINGBOARD

Kike Oniwinde, BYP Network

Kike is a Forbes 30 Under 30 entrepreneur, and has been a high achiever since she was raised in East London, throwing the javelin for Great Britain while excelling at school with her grades.

In 2020, she raised £900,000 through crowdfunding for her business, BYP Network: a platform that empowers and connects Black professionals to each other and to corporations. But it was her participation in an accelerator programme, and entering pitch competitions, that gave her the initial springboard in funding her business:

> *'BYP always was revenue-generating from the get-go from event ticket sales. I kept reinvesting that same money for the next event. The thing is, I didn't know that there was any other way – I didn't know you could raise money.*
>
> *Then it was like, "What do I do next, or how do I go from here?" That's how I entered the whole entrepreneurial scene. I joined New Entrepreneurs Foundation, and through them I connected to a lot of other entrepreneurs, investors, learned a bit more about the whole fundraising and growth journey.*

At the end of that, that's when I won their pitch competition. I also won the Founders of the Future pitch competition, and a Sky scholarship as a Future Woman in Technology. I think you should just go for whichever pitch events you see. It's good to practise.

I won about £40,000 from those three competitions. I think they were in the same week as well, so that was like a triple whammy of high-end visibility, for sure.

I then went full-time because I'm like, "What the hell, I need to focus on this business." Then that's when the networking started. I started off with a very strong base off the back of those pitch competitions: through them, I met four angels who invested £150,000 in my pre-seed round.'

Reach out to investors

The goal in approaching investors is to secure a meeting with those people who are likely to be a good fit. Getting a meeting with a potential investor is invaluable, as this enables you to really understand their needs and drivers, build a relationship, trust and confidence, and have a proper two-way conversation about the opportunity.

In a meeting, you can deal with questions and concerns on the spot, put things in context and fully demonstrate your competence and flair as an entrepreneurial leader – we'll be covering this in more detail in Step 5 (Chapter 9).

Use your well-crafted email template or message that you developed in Step 3 to engage interest, pre-qualify and make it easy to for the *right* investors to want to meet with you – where possible, using the person who introduced you as a hook.

As previously mentioned, it also can be helpful to send your teaser deck with this email, ideally linking to a digital version stored in the cloud, so you can track views and control distribution tightly. Your teaser deck is enough for them to understand whether the business might be a good fit.

Again, as we touched on in Step 3, don't send your main pitch deck with *all* the information about your business with an introductory email. This risks a potentially great investor making their mind up without having a meeting with you: either you won't hear back from them at all, or they'll come back to you with a brush-off that doesn't really tell you *why* they don't want to back you – which isn't very helpful.

Some angel syndicates, funds and VCs have a standard application process for start-ups on their websites. Do follow these, but also try and connect with individuals at the organisations too, where possible: take a belt-and-braces approach.

Run your campaign

When you're busy building a high-growth potential business, it's very easy for your fundraising campaign to slip down to the bottom of your to-do list. The following approach will help you remain focused and efficient.

Set daily outreach targets

When you're activating your existing network – especially if it's large – one option is to send out an email en masse, as this saves you a lot of time.

However, segment your database if you can, and tailor the message accordingly. If you have a smaller list, it can be worth the extra effort to personalise each message and target, reaching out to five people per day.

Put time in your diary weekly for investor meetings

Aim for first meetings to be via video conferencing: it's more efficient than in-person, which can take half a day of your time, including travel. Use a calendar scheduling tool to reduce admin overload. Second meetings with qualified investors who have shown interest are worth doing in person, where possible.

Track your fundraising activity and progress thoroughly
Be clear where investor follow-up is needed and what action to take next – setting firm deadlines, and accountability for follow-up – so nothing falls through the gaps. You can do this on a simple spreadsheet or online project management tool.

STORY: A MILITARY APPROACH

Heinin Zhang, YHangry

After working together on the trading floor at Barclays, Heinin and her co-founder Siddhi Mittal became firm friends through their shared passion to become entrepreneurs.

Going out to restaurants four to five times a week, they realised how much they were missing quality time at home with friends over a dinner party, but didn't have the time or skills to host one. So they established YHangry as a private chef service at an affordable price, offering an in-home, complete service to take the hard work out of entertaining.

In a short space of time, demand exploded. Heinin and Siddhi quit their jobs to go full-time, put together a very detailed plan to execute their fundraising goals, and raised more than £1 million.

Here's how Heinin got organised:

> *'First, we created a Notion page, which we called "weekly strategy breakdown", where we wrote down certain assumptions: for example, how much we wanted to raise. Then we created a weekly plan, which was week 1, week 2, week 3, week 4. By week 4 we wanted to have £800,000 committed, and be done.*

We were super-methodical in looking at and identifying potential angel investors: we researched anyone who'd invested in European or UK marketplaces or food tech businesses within the past three years; then we looked at founders of marketplaces and looked at whether they invest, and created our prospective investor list of 200 investors, which we ranked in order of relevance.

Siddhi and I decided to divide and conquer – which is the best decision we made, as it helped us to raise within weeks. Otherwise, for one person to operate at that level of intensity when it comes to calls and doing work, and integrating feedback and improving things, it's just not sustainable. Fundraising is emotionally and psychologically taxing.

Classifying investors helped us digest a "Yes" versus a "No". Instead of feeling down because someone gave us a "No", analysing and realising this investor is completely irrelevant, maybe because they don't understand the sector, really helped. We didn't reach out to all the people on our list, because we started getting traction and introductions. I would say we spoke to maybe 50 people each.

It was like a sprint rather than a marathon, although you never know which way it's going to go when you start.'

You might expect to have between 11 and 30 meetings, if not more, during your fundraising campaign.[16] As you might imagine, this is time-consuming, so the more tightly you can run the process, the better.

Have faith. If you make it a priority to reach out to investors every day with effective communication messages, and manage the process tightly and with urgency, before long you'll be making lots of high-quality investor connections which have the potential to fund your business.

Action steps

1. Get really clear on the profile of investors you'd like to have on board: how much involvement you want them to have, and the skills, experience, connections and further money they might bring. Make a note of this before you start reaching out to investors, as it's good to refer back to later.
2. Understand whether your business has unicorn potential and might appeal to a VC, and whether you'd be prepared to go down that 'do or die' route to investment, scaling hard-and-fast. If not, look for more patient capital elsewhere.
3. Consider how much investment you need and how far along your growth journey your start-up is: cross-reference this against which types of investors might be appropriate for where you sit right now in terms of the funding they have available, and their risk profile.
4. Start with your network. Build a list of everyone you know – it might already be there in your electronic contacts list, or on LinkedIn. Don't assume people won't want to invest before you've given them the opportunity.
5. Lock yourself away for a few hours to do some desk research on other investors with whom you might want to connect. Brainstorm ideas about the types of investors; think as laterally as possible. Then, search online to find good candidates.
6. Use your existing network to help you connect with new people, and get introductions and referrals where you can. Again, LinkedIn is a helpful tool for this.

7. Set yourself some clear targets on how much outreach activity you'll do each day or week, to keep you moving forward at pace.
8. Focus on getting meetings to put you in front of your ideal investor in person (or via online video). Use calendar scheduling to arrange meetings to save time and energy.
9. Keep track of all your investor outreach activity and how conversations are progressing using a spreadsheet, CRM system or an online project management tool.

9
Step 5: Commitment – investor meetings

Finally, after all your hard work preparing your fundraising campaign, reaching out to investors and scheduling meetings in the diary, you find yourself in front of whom you hope will be your ideal investor.

You're ready to pitch your business and secure commitment on funding.

Before we go any further, let's put aside the idea that this is a pitch. Instead, think of your investor meeting as a conversation: a two-way discussion that's structured cleverly, so both parties get what they need from it – which is a decision. Without a decision, investor discussions can drag on, and your energy and resources quickly become depleted. Having lots of conversations that lead nowhere, or keep you hanging on outcomes, can be a real waste of your time.

There's no doubt about it, an investor meeting can feel like the conversation of a lifetime: the difference between a 'Yes' and a 'No' for funding can have a huge impact on whether your business can move forward and scale... or not. Knowing this can create a lot of fear and anxiety, which can mean you don't perform at your best if your emotions aren't managed well.

Remember, these are people just like you, who are doing their job – which is investing in exciting new start-ups. They need you as much as you need them! Try to relax, don't allow yourself to feel intimidated by the situation, and remember the techniques we covered in Chapter 4 for building confidence and a strong mindset.

In this final step of the fundraising process, we'll look at how to structure investor meetings so you can make the most of them, and have the best chance of securing commitment quickly. Then we'll move on to the process of getting your deal closed.

The RUSC approach

A well-structured investor meeting can be broken down into four distinct stages that – when executed well – take you naturally through the process of determining if an investment deal would be mutually-beneficial for both you and your investor, and secure their commitment to moving forward.

I define these stages with the RUSC acronym:

1. **Rapport** – build trust and a connection with your investor, and set the framework for the meeting.
2. **Understand** – get to know what your investor's problems are, what they want and need, and check whether they're the right fit for you.
3. **Solve** – run the investor through your pitch to show them how it solves their problems, wants and needs.
4. **Close** – ask the investor if they'd like to invest, deal with any concerns or objections they might have, and if they're in, confirm their commitment.

Let's explore each of these in more detail.

Rapport

Rapport is a close and harmonious relationship in which the people or groups concerned understand each other's feelings or ideas, and communicate well.

If you have rapport with your investors, you'll be much more able to have an open and honest conversation about the investment opportunity, and whether you might be a good fit for one another. Building a strong level of trust and mutual respect as soon as possible is important, particularly as people do business with people they like.

How do you build rapport quickly, if you don't already know this investor?

- The most effective technique to find common ground is to ask friendly, genuine questions, and really listen to the answers.
- If you've done your research, you might be able to ask about articles they've published, industry conferences they've been at, recent investments they've made or contacts you have in common.
- You might also chat about more personal things, such as where they live, their family or what they enjoy doing.

Make sure you've got this rapport going a little before you move on, as it helps both you and your investor relax.

At this stage, it's also helpful to establish how the meeting will go. Check how much time the investor has, and explain that you'd like to understand more about their investment objectives before you talk through your business in more detail.

STORY: DIALOGUE, NOT MONOLOGUE

Mrs Riham Satti, MeVitae

A self-confessed 'accidental entrepreneur', women-in-tech advocate Riham is a neuroscientist and two-time postgraduate. She's also co-founder of MeVitae, a tech company that uses big data and machine learning to tackle unconscious bias in the world of recruitment.

Riham took MeVitae through four years of development and research with grant funding before swapping academia for the fundraising arena. In 2018 she kickstarted the company's growth with a £500,000 raise that brought in angels and VC investors plus plenty of learnings, including how to have great conversations with investors.

> *'Introductions, introductions, introductions – that was the most efficient and warmer way of reaching investors. And building a relationship was key. It's not about, "We're raising £500,000, can you give us £500,000?" It's about whether we fit together as a start-up and for them as a firm or an angel, because they're going to be on your board. They're going to be working with you for not just one year, but five, 10 years potentially. It's around building that connection, and making sure you do that along the way.*
>
> *Most of it's about listening too: it's way more than talking. It's making sure you answer their questions, try to understand their body language and what excites them, what doesn't. It really is an art of preparation, communication and body language.*
>
> *All the investors we brought on board we've either known for several years or through introductions where the relationship was built over just a week or two. We love all our investors to bits – they've just been phenomenal.'*

Understand

Ask any professional investor, in the hundreds of investment pitches they've heard over the years, when do they remember a single founder asking what would motivate them to invest? It happens very rarely – and that is a huge mistake.

If you don't know what's important to your prospective investor, how can you possibly know if they're a good fit for you? No two investors are alike, or look at an opportunity in exactly the same way, so you can't assume what's important to them. Before you start to talk through your start-up, make sure you first understand each prospective investor's specific mix of motivations.

How do we understand our investor? By asking open, strategic questions tailored to the type of investor they are and their investing experience. Those questions also help to go deeper into rapport, demonstrate your authority and expertise, and differentiate you from most of the entrepreneurs they see.

People love to feel understood and listened to, so focusing on them helps you have more control within the conversation.

Here are some good opening questions:

- Which sectors and industries do you prefer to invest in?
- What challenges do you face when deciding where to invest?
- What concerns do you have when you're investing in start-ups?

If you get superficial answers, be curious and keep probing until you find out what's really motivating them. For example:

- Why do you think that is?
- Why do you feel that way?

- Why is that important to you?

Or:

- That's interesting. Tell me more about that...
- What's been the impact of that for you?
- How do you feel about that?

Don't put words into their mouth: get them to tell you. As you explore your investor's challenges and problems in more depth, every question leads to the next, so it flows like a conversation.

Unless it's very clearly stated on the investor's website, you also need to be clear about the typical commercials they're looking for on a deal. You might ask:

- What stage of venture deals do you tend to come in on?
- What deal size do you usually look for?
- What is your valuation sweet spot?
- What is your typical investment amount in a start-up?
- Are you able to follow on with your money?
- Do you prefer to lead on a deal, be the sole investor or co-invest?

These questions will really help you not only to understand what's important to your potential investor, but whether they're a good fit for you. If you don't think they're a fit, you may as well politely end the conversation there.

STORY: THE INVESTOR DATING GAME

Ilana Lever and Cecily Motley, Motley London

Longstanding friends and co-founders Cecily and Ilana brought together 20 years' experience in consumer goods and high-end jewellery to form Motley London, a platform that brings consumers exclusively designed, affordable jewellery from the world's leading designers, disrupting a long-outmoded sector.

They likened finding investors that were the right fit to being a dating game, when they raised £365,000 after a year of being in business.

> *'It was a relief when we met one of our early investors, who is a director of e-commerce. He got it immediately, he was like:*
>
> *"Jewellery is a massive growth industry but quite slow to come online, so I really understand what you're doing."*
>
> *The other thing that helped were two small-ticket investors [investors who put in relatively small amounts of investment] that are very successful direct-to-consumer entrepreneurs, who really got our customer demographic. In the end we had 22 angel investors: we didn't mind having that many, because by letting people in on small tickets, we gained amazing expertise that we wouldn't have had otherwise.*
>
> *Interestingly, a venture capital fund did offer us the full round. We decided to turn them down, which was sort of terrifying – but it just felt wrong. First, they wanted to be the sole investor, which would have meant losing all the expertise of the angels who wanted to back us. But they were also obsessed with one of us being CEO.*
>
> *We said, "We have a very collaborative relationship. We have a very clear division of responsibilities." They kept pushing and pushing and said, "How do you make decisions?*

You need one person to make decisions." Now reflecting on it, we wish we'd said, "Well, how do families work?"

It seems a very male concept to have one chief, but as founders we come from quite different perspectives. When we disagree on something, what we normally come out with is way better than either of our opinions in the first place. Culture is king: to try and mess with that is a very dangerous and unnecessary thing. It didn't feel right for a VC to try to impose certain types of behaviour that they think are start-up behaviours – but are actually male behaviours.

Their desire to create some hierarchy between us also made us a bit nervous. We knew that it was an issue, because we asked the question:

"If we are delivering the growth that we expect to deliver, would you still put pressure on us to have a sole CEO?"

They said, "Yes."

When you get an answer like that, you're like, "Well, if you are that stuck in your ways and you're that cookie-cutter, you're not the right partner for us."

Solve

Once you have a good understanding of your investor and what's important to them, you can move on to talk through your business and frame the value of investing.

An experienced investor is trying to pick a winner: they're placing a bet, and they'll be calculating the risk involved. Your job is to demonstrate how you will solve their problem, and minimise any risks they perceive.

This part of the meeting is where you can run through your pitch deck, position each part of your investment story in terms of what's important to this particular investor, and check for understanding and agreement along the way. There's no need to rush: bring your investor along with you as you walk through your narrative, and deal with any concerns or reservations they might have as they come up.

Keep your questions curious and open, to find out what they think.

Here are just a couple of examples. Once you've explained the problem you're addressing in the market, you could ask:

- Do you see how this is a real problem that people face?
- Is this something you have personal experience of, or that resonates with you?

Once you've run through your product or service offering, you can check to see if you're both on the same page:

- We believe we're really solving our customer's problems in a way that's better than anything out there, so we can truly make a difference. What do you think?
- Do you have any concerns about it at all?

When you've explained the traction you've achieved so far, you might ask:

- Given the progress we've already made, we believe this proves we can make it work and the potential really is there. What are your thoughts on that?
- Although we've still got things to prove out, we think we've de-risked the opportunity a lot. Do you agree?

– and so on, as you move through the pitch deck to present your plan.

Always bring it back to the investor:

- Do they get it?
- Can you show that this is a fit for them and solves their problems?
- Are they on board so far?

If they're not, it can be a real struggle to move on with the rest of the story, and they're probably not a fit.

Pay attention and listen closely, as their interactions with you will help to shape your story. Look out for their body language, such as nodding or the look in their eyes, and verbal queues such as little noises or questions. This guides you on how to make your story relatable and exciting for them.

STORY: TALKING TAMPONS WITH INVESTORS

Martha Silcott, FabLittleBag

FabLittleBag is a sustainably sourced, feminine hygiene product disposal bag that not only solves the perpetual problem that women have of what to do with used period products, but also at its heart addresses the significant environmental issues that come with people flushing these products down the loo.

The inventor and founder of the business, Martha, raised £400,000 in equity funding from angel investors after a few years of growing the company. But pitching a period product to male investors required a very different approach.

> *'The subject matter was very tricky, because when you walk into a room of investors and the vast majority, if not all, are men – and usually, frankly, middle-aged men – you've got to get straight in there talking about tampons, sanitary towels, periods,*

gloopy drips – the whole thing. It's not their fault they don't understand what you're talking about on an empathetic basis.

I really had to address that very quickly, and give them some facts and figures to warm them up. And then I'd get straight in there and allow them to feel how it feels being a 'binner' when you haven't got a perfect binning environment around you.

I'd get them to perch on the end of their chair and give them a tampon or sanitary towel – a new one, obviously! – and a loo roll, and say: "OK, so there's your loo roll, there's your dangling tampon, wrap it up, now put that in your briefcase!" And they'd struggle, as you do. Then we'd give them FabLittleBag and ask them to do the same.

Making investors experience a little bit of what it's like, helped them understand it more. And they'd inevitably go home and start talking about it with their girlfriend, wife, daughter, and that's when they got really excited – when they got the feedback saying, "Yes, it is horrible, I really hate that bit." They're like, "Wow, I never knew!"

Where there's a disconnect with a natural empathy, you need to create that experience as best you can – and then hopefully they will enhance that with direct conversations with women they feel comfortable talking to about it.'

Don't move on until you feel you've really nailed the 'solve' part of the meeting, as there is no point in trying to secure commitment from an investor until you're sure they're on board. Selling something before the buyer is ready to buy never works.

If you feel they're on the same page and interested, then you can move on to the final part of the meeting, which is where you are going to close the investor.

Close

Closing the investor is simply the next step in a normal conversation: you shouldn't feel stressed about this, because if you've done your job well in the meeting so far, it should be starting to feel reasonably clear whether the person in front of you is keen to invest.

The thing to do now is create some pull rather than push, which raises your value and authority. Show the investor that you're picky about who you work with, so that they effectively sell themselves to *you*.

Remember, you have standards and you want to work with the best. You're not here with a begging bowl!

In closing the investor, first walk them through your investment offer. Explain:

- how much you're raising
- your timescales
- the overall terms
- what you're looking for in investors.

Then do a final check for fit by asking a question along the following lines:

- It's important to us that we get the right fit with investors who come on board, because this needs to be a long-term, mutually-beneficial relationship. Now that we've been through the plan, how do you feel our interests are aligned?
- What value do you feel you could add as an investor in our business?

- If I were to speak with other founders you've backed, what do you think they would tell me about what it's like to have you as an investor?

If you're happy that the fit is good, then simply ask the question:

'Would you be interested in investing?'

At this point they're going to say, 'No', 'Maybe' or 'Yes'.

Dealing with 'No'

Often, the decision will be a 'No' because the fit isn't good. That's OK, because you only want to work with those investors where the fit is perfect, and not make any compromises. It's far better to get an honest refusal, rather than leading yourself to believe the investor is in when they really aren't.

And if you get yourself into a mindset of seeing every 'No' as taking you one step closer to a 'Yes' from someone else, it won't feel so bad.

If 'No' is the case:

- Find out *why* – it might be that the investor feels you're not quite at the right stage for them yet, and they'd like to see more progress. Or they might have more fundamental concerns, which could be invaluable feedback. Whether or not you agree with their comments, listen carefully and thank them for sharing their insights.
- Find out if they would be interested in staying in touch with a view to potentially investing later – if there's a possibility of becoming the right fit for them in the future. Then you can keep them on your communications list, and update them regularly on your progress to nurture the relationship over time.

- Ask them if there are any other investors they know where the fit might be better – and if they'd consider introducing you. In this way, you continue to build out your network, and might discover the perfect investor through that referral.

Dealing with 'Maybe'

There's no such thing as a 'Maybe', because anything other than a 'Yes' is basically a 'No'.

The most important thing here is to bring the investor to a point of decision. Don't fool yourself into thinking that someone will get back to you when they say they will, because it's very common for a founder to come away from an investor meeting saying the investor is in... only to find out later that they really aren't.

This complexity is based on two dynamics:

- founders have happy ears – always thinking the most positive and optimistic outcome
- investors don't want to miss out – they like the option of being in the round.

This dynamic isn't great for founders, because when investors do drop out of a fundraising round due to lack of firm commitment, the whole round can fall apart.

If the investor isn't sure or says they need time to think, it means the investor is not there *yet*. They need a little more reassurance.

- Ask what their concerns or objections are – so you can deal with them there and then if you can. Your job here is to dig under the surface of that 'Maybe', and find out what's really going on.
- The investor may want further information to help address their concerns – if so, ask them what they need to be able

to facilitate their decision. If you have that information now, share it with them while you're in the meeting.

- When people ask you to send over information so they can review it in their own time, this can be a delaying tactic and a way of getting themselves out of the meeting or off the call, because they're just not sure yet. If you let them go, it can become much harder subsequently to find out why they didn't invest.
- If they insist you send further documents so they can review them in their own time, first check: 'Assuming you're happy with the documents sent, are there any other concerns you have about making this investment? Is there any other information you need?'
- Don't leave it open-ended – agree a commitment on timings for next steps, which ideally is another meeting or phone call to follow up.

Dealing with 'Yes'

If you get a 'Yes', then great news! Remember though, the deal's not done yet.

- Ask how much they want to invest. Their commitment on this will help to reassure you that their interest is potentially real.
- Check to see if there are any conditions for this money being invested, as you need to know this now. For example, they might only want to come in once you have a lead investor confirmed, or there might be a particular date after which they will have money available.
- Repeat back what they've said verbally, celebrate the decision with them, then confirm the next steps: that you will send them a confirmation email following the meeting.

- Send your confirmation email straight after the meeting, and ask them to reply confirming their understanding. Although there is nothing legally binding about these emails, having it in writing is essential to get greater compliance with their commitment.

Overcome gender bias

In Chapter 2 we looked at how investors tend to venturesplain to female founders, as well as ask them more questions which are preventative in nature.

How we deal with these challenges is important. When we feel threatened, our reaction might be one of flight, fight or freeze. But becoming aggressive or defensive, running out of the room or doing nothing are unlikely to serve us well in this situation – and might perpetuate the old investor world viewpoint that women 'aren't really up to it'.

Let's now consider how to deal with these challenges in a productive way, using your intelligence and smarts to open the investor's eyes to what you have to offer as a female founder – and perhaps to their own prejudices in the process.

Deal with venturesplaining

Here are some tactics which can be very effective at stopping venturesplaining in its tracks and switch the focus back to you:

- Challenge their expertise with grace. For example, you might say: 'Thanks for your views. Could you tell me more about your specific experience in this area that's led you to think that?'
- Step in and tell them why you're qualified, with a statement such as: 'I wonder if I could stop you there? I'd really like to share with you some more about my experience on this issue.'

- Use humour to switch it up in a non-aggressive way, with a gentle prod such as: 'Have you heard of the term 'mansplaining'? I kind of feel like I might have been mansplained to a little just then! I wonder, could I tell you more about what I've learned about this area over my years working on this?'

(Note that this approach is only for the brave! It needs to be done with the right level of cheekiness, not to rile the other party.)

Always make sure you strongly emphasise your credibility and knowledge. Blowing our own trumpet may not come naturally to all of us, and many female founders worry about coming across as too arrogant. There's no need to feel that way, as long as you're speaking about yourself in a genuine, authentic manner – this is not the time to hide your light under a bushel. As you showcase what you're really made of, the chances are you'll win them over.

And if you don't? Well, it's their loss. Quite frankly, if this is how a person makes you feel in an initial meeting, do you really want them on board in your business?

Smile, nod your head and swiftly leave!

STORY: A FEMALE-ONLY INVESTMENT ROUND

Bonnie Lister Parsons, School of SOS
Bonnie's dance career boast credits including One Direction, Florence and The Machine and *X Factor Live*. At the height of this success, she founded School of SOS to get the dancers we see on screen into classes for professional women looking for an empowering workout.

But speaking with male investors proved harder than she had thought, when she went out on her first investment raise for £100,000.

> *'In the early days of raising money, I didn't consciously see investors as "male", or have any context around the sexism in the investment community. I just saw these powerful, influential men I was meeting with as opportunities. I would have a great meeting with them and then they would take it back to their VC partners, but they would come back to me and say, "It's great, but you're too early."*
>
> *Then I started to notice that I seemed to always be "too early", while male founders were raising money on the back of ideas and PowerPoint presentations with zero traction. So I started to ask myself, "Why am I too early, but he isn't?"*
>
> *I think that's where the unconscious bias comes in. Not one of the male investors I met were bad people. But I think seeing a young woman makes some people go "No" in the gut. I think they just looked at me and thought, "I don't believe she can pull it off."*
>
> *But what I had done is proven I could build a customer base of thousands. I could get recommended by every publication under the sun. I could do it profitably. And I could generate six-figure revenues on my own. The penny dropped, and I was like:*
>
> *"It's because I don't look like Mark Zuckerberg."*
>
> *Then the rage sets in and then the stubborn, ruthless determination to do it sets in – and then you keep going.*
>
> *So I decided to raise an all-female investment round instead. I published an article about it, which also went out on social media, then I saw these emails saying, "I've just seen your post and I'm really interested in investing."*

I guess I'd put myself out there and put my money where my mouth was really because I had to, I didn't have any other choice – but the pieces fell into place from there.

I found women had been looking to invest for a long time, and they wanted to invest. They just didn't know where to find a business or a founder they believed in.'

Table 8: VCs frame questions in two different ways[1]

Topic	Promotion	Prevention
Customers	Acquisition Example question: 'How do you want to acquire customers?'	Retention Example question: 'How many daily and monthly active users do you have?'
Income statement	Sales 'How do you plan to monetise this?'	Margins 'How long will it take you to break even?'
Market	Size 'Do you think that your target market is a growing one'?	Share 'Is it a defensible business wherein other people can't come into the space to take share?'
Projections	Growth 'What major milestones are you targeting for this year?'	Stability 'How predictable are your future cash flows?'
Strategy	Vision 'What's the brand vision?'	Execution 'Are you planning to Turing Test this?'
Management	Entrepreneur 'Can you tell us a bit about yourself?'	Team 'How much of this are you actually doing in-house?'

Source: Table reproduced by kind permission of *Harvard Business Review*. Originally published under the English title, 'Male and female entrepreneurs get asked different questions by VCs – and it affects how much funding they get', by Dana Kanze, Laura Huang, Mark A. Conley and E. Tory Higgins, in the issue June 2017.

Handle prevention questions

Prevention questions that focus on potential losses, as opposed to potential gains, can crop up across all areas that investors might question you on. The key is to spot when it's happening, so you can address it. Table 8 above summarises some of the differences to look out for.

When you spot a prevention question, the trick is to reframe the answers to give promotion answers. It's worth practising this in advance: writing out all those difficult questions you're afraid of, and scope out exactly how you'll answer them. The more you do this, the easier and more natural it will become.

By way of example: if you're asked about how you'll defend your start-up's market share, frame your response around the size and growth potential of the overall market, rather than just talking about how you're going to protect your share of it.

STORY: FLIPPING THE CONVERSATION

Hele Väärsi, 9Plus1

9Plus1 is an innovative start-up in the growing space of apparel rental and sustainable fashion, focusing on baby clothes.

Hele raised £300,000 from a female-focused fund early on after founding the business, when she and her co-founder were still at the idea stage. Hele strategically contacted VCs whom she thought might have an interest in the product, but found the questions she was asked rather challenging, to say the least.

> *'I have a male co-founder, but I tried to hold most of those investor talks because first, I'm stubborn enough, and if it's important to an investor whether a company is founded by men or women, I'm not sure I want to work with you. I try to prove to myself or anyone else that I can do it, without having*

to bring my male founder in and having him taking those talks simply because he's a man.

Although some male investors really understood the business, we had a lot of: "What's the market? Is there a market? It's a niche market only." Niche market?! Everyone has been a baby one day. I'm pretty sure most of us babies were wearing clothes!

I felt the conversations I had with male VCs were also very different because I'm a woman. When I was asked why haven't we launched already, I tried to explain we needed a certain amount of stock, certain type of machines – we need funding first. Being told then, "How about you start from a spare bedroom?"

I don't want to start from a spare bedroom! If I was a man, would you tell a man, "Come on, slow down and start from your spare bedroom. You're very small, and prove to me that you can do it – then we will talk or not."

Or being asked, "What's the plan if you're going to fail?" I don't want to fail!

Or, "If you have to take higher risks, would you be willing to take those higher risks?" My answer being that I first need to know all the criteria to decide – that wasn't good enough because, obviously most men would probably answer, "Yes, I would take the risk."

If you can recognise the question, you can flip it, but still it can get stuck in the back of your head and put the brakes on for you. You start questioning yourself.

The only way we can get rid of that is to stop those questions. We must start asking the same questions from female founders and male founders.'

Address pregnancy and children

There are countless female founders who've successfully raised an investment round while pregnant, about to give birth, from their hospital bed or surrounded by toddlers and nappies.

It's more than possible, although that doesn't mean it's easy. On the one hand, if you're pregnant and considering raising investment, you may wish to factor this into the timing of your round, as it's going to be hard work and fairly stressful. On the other hand, fundraising while pregnant shows huge commitment and drive.

Don't let other people's fears and judgements influence how you feel and what you want to do.

If you're about to have a baby, there is likely to be a period where you'll be off the radar to a certain extent – and understandably, investors might want to know more about how you plan to run the business during this time. Beyond that, the issue should be no different than it would be for any parent with small children. Male entrepreneurs with new babies also suffer from sleepless nights, and need to prioritise the children over work from time to time too. That's life!

The right investors will understand this. If they don't, again, you might want to question whether they're the right fit for you.

STORY: THE POWER OF MOTHERHOOD

Emily Bendell, Bluebella

Lingerie: not the typical career route for an Oxford Politics, Philosophy and Economics grad. Emily stood out from the crowd, took her degree and built an underwear business made for and by women, along the way raising investment from an all-female investor group as well as through crowdfunding.

Emily has steered the business into international and profitable success, doubling in growth every year and now a multi-million-pound turnover business, while also raising a young family.

'I've had investor meetings when I've been raising with angels, before I had children, who asked about my plans for starting a family – which would be illegal in a job interview and would never be asked of male entrepreneurs. I think there were plenty of investors who weren't enlightened about that. I wouldn't want investment from somebody that thought that was an appropriate question to ask.

I think in taking investment, you have to have the same shared hopes and dreams and go to work together, otherwise it's just going to end in disaster.

I'm not immune to worrying about what investors think. One of the perks for our crowdfunding investors was to come to a champagne reception. When I found out I was pregnant, I was like:

"We've got to get this thing done quick. I don't want to turn up with a big bump."

I didn't want to freak them all out.

For me – and I genuinely mean this – I've been more effective since I had a child, in the sense that I've become so ruthless with my time, as it's so precious. Once you have a child, you look carefully at everything you're doing, and consider whether it's right that you're even doing it.

I started to empower my team to do things I probably should have empowered them to do ages ago and hadn't, because I'm a bit of a control freak! These are things that I have not taken back, once I've been back in full swing in the business.

I think people should stop seeing having a young family as being difficult to manage, and understand that it helps hone your skills – it's really positive.'

In conclusion, investor meetings don't need to be as scary as you might think. Step into them with the right mindset, and see them as an opportunity to find a potential backer who's the right fit for you, where the balance of power isn't skewed.

If you structure and control the flow of the discussion and deal effectively with questions, you should quickly get to the natural conclusion of knowing either that this is not the right partnership (or at least, not for now), or firmly securing commitment.

Once you have that initial 'Yes', you'll be ready to get to work on securing the rest of the investment you need and closing your fundraising round.

Action steps

1. See investor meetings as a conversation, not a pitch, and follow the RUSC approach on how to structure your time with them: Rapport, Understand, Solve, Close.
2. Build trust and connection with your investor by doing your research in advance, asking questions and listening.
3. Ensure you understand your investor well to figure out if they could be a good fit, again by asking questions – what is their investment thesis, their experience in investing, and what are they looking for?
4. Take your investor through your pitch step-by-step, checking for understanding and agreement along the way to show

them how you'll solve their problems. Address concerns as they come up.

5. Allow the investor space to sell themselves to you, to elevate your authority and credibility.
6. If the investor says 'No' or 'Maybe', dig to fully understand what their objections are – you may be able to address them or deepen your own understanding of potential issues.
7. Be on the lookout for venturesplaining and prevention questions, as well as any questions around pregnancy or childcare, and consider how you might address them if this happens to you.
8. If the investor is in, clarify and confirm verbally, followed by written email confirmation both ways.

10
Step 5: Commitment – close your deal

Getting your first investor committed is one thing. Closing the round and getting your deal over the line is another thing altogether: it's an art and a science, and every deal comes together differently. Nobody wants to spend their whole life fundraising, so the aim is to get it done efficiently, effectively and quickly.

Your lead investor typically oversees the process of agreeing your term sheet, undertaking due diligence and your final deal paperwork, which we'll be looking at shortly in this chapter.

If you have a lead investor committed who will complete the whole round – i.e. invest all the money you need – and if you like them and are happy with the broad terms of the deal, then great news! But the chances are, you may need a few or several investors to complete your round, or indeed to have enough commitment before you crowdfund, if you're pursuing that strategy. Also, you might wish to shop your deal around to get the best terms.

Your job now is to secure those other investors, and get your deal over the line. Committed investors can pull out at any point before they sign the final paperwork, and it's dangerous to put all your eggs in one basket – so keep speaking to other potential backers until you have the money in the bank.

STORY: STRENGTH THROUGH SETBACKS

Julianne Ponan, Creative Nature

Julianne's superfood brand, Creative Nature, creates raw superfoods, snacks and food mixes suitable for everyone, including those who are nutrition-conscious, vegans and who live with a food allergy or intolerance.

Her first attempt at raising investment didn't lead to the success she was hoping for. But after she landed a major contract with a supermarket giant, she was ready to brave the fundraising arena once more – and her renewed confidence led her to seek investment through crowdfunding again.

This time, Julianne raised more than £500,000, smashing her target of £350,000.

> *'When I first tried crowdfunding, I failed. I'd never run a crowdfunding campaign before, so I didn't really know what to do. I think the fact that I didn't have a full marketing plan in place didn't help things. When I launched on the platform, I didn't have any investment lined up, so the momentum wasn't there. We didn't do the video well, we didn't have the budget to do it. Obviously, that's why we were funding, but you do need to make sure certain things come across authentic and are done to a professional level at the same time.*
>
> *It was difficult to deal with that setback. That's when I wanted to throw in the towel. I felt like I'd had enough – that this wasn't for me and I couldn't take it any further. But my then partner (and now husband) said to me:*
>
> *"Think about why you started this in the first place."*

That was the key driver: the mission, the ethos.

Together, we came up with a plan on how to get the business to the next level without investment, growing the business organically and funding it all through profit. This put us in a much stronger position when we went out to crowdfund for the second time.

We put our target at £350,000 and we had around £250,000 pledged in advance, but it wasn't guaranteed. There were people that dropped out. You need to make sure you've got an extra buffer in there just in case, because some people will say, "Yes, I will definitely be putting in £100,000" and that's a lot of money. Then if you suddenly have that one person pull out, you don't have any back-up.

Until your deal is closed, it's meaningless. We had more than 400 investors in the end, which is great. These are people who can help us get our brand to the next level by going out there, buying it and spreading the word.'

Timelines and leverage

It's important your deal doesn't do the rounds in the investment ecosystem for too long, otherwise it's going to start looking a bit tired: you need to keep your deal fresh. This is especially true if you're talking to well-known professional angels who are active in the industry, or with early-stage VCs: these people all talk to each other, so will become aware that your deal is out there. The last thing you want is for investors to feel like your business has been rejected by too many other parties, because you've been trying to raise for so long.

Ideally, you want to get your deal done within a month or two, once you've started speaking with investors. There's a huge amount of psychology involved in getting your round closed. Even though investors will tell you they make their own decisions and aren't influenced by others, as we saw previously they absolutely hate to miss out on a good deal, and you can use this to your advantage:

- **Set timelines** – make them definite enough that investors feel some pressure to commit, but don't set them so tight and fixed that you'll get egg on your face if you haven't made it happen by then.
- **Communicate these timelines to other potential investors** – depending on where you are in the process, you can say something like, 'We're aiming to get this completed by the end of the month/in the next few weeks' or similar.
- **Keep all committed parties warm** – during this period where you're closing the round, maintain regular communication: not just on how the deal is coming together, but also on key business milestones and positive news.
- **Name drop** – if your lead investor is well known and has an excellent reputation, with their permission you can use their name as a hook for others to join the round.
- **Leverage your committed investors to get more investors** – after a couple of days of their commitment to your round, reach out and ask if there are one or two other investors they may be able to introduce you to: the introductions that come from committed investors are always very powerful.

The more investors that commit to your round, the faster it will progress, because momentum is built through a network effect (as we saw in Chapter 8).

STORY: KEEPING IT FRESH

Sophie Baron, Mamamade

Going back to work after having her first baby, Sophie struggled to find baby food she felt was good enough, so to fill the gap Mamamade was born in March 2019, providing fresh, frozen, nutritious homemade baby meals directly to their customers' door.

Sophie bootstrapped the business for around a year before embarking on her angel funding round for £300,000, closing her round within just three months, and has since gone on to raise a further round for £1.5 million.

> *'We started our fundraising campaign during lockdown in 2020, as this was a huge period of growth for us. Fundraising becomes a full-time job, but video calls with investors made it quicker, because there wasn't any travel time. You don't want your campaign to get stale because if things don't seem like they're moving, that's just not as attractive to an investor – we wanted to keep the pace up.*
>
> *It was just a crazy process, because on top of that we were in lockdown, our daughter wasn't yet back at nursery, it was a period of insane growth for the business and I was in my first trimester being pregnant – so it was just a very rollercoaster experience.*
>
> *I took ownership of my own schedule: on certain days I would take investor meetings, and other days I would purely focus on the business. The first few investors were the hardest. Towards the end, we got a lot more "yeses" a lot quicker, because people started to see the round was filling up.*
>
> *We set a firm deadline for people. We knew we needed to close it by then, however much we were going to close at: that was*

partly because we just needed to get the funds in, and didn't want it to drag out.

Overall, we had probably hundreds of people look at the deck, followed by maybe 20–30 productive Zoom conversations, leading, to in the end, about 10–15 investors.

At one point I thought we'd be closing at £100,000, so the fact that we closed at almost three times that was a nice surprise.'

Agree your term sheet

Your term sheet is the key document that captures all the basics of the investment deal. It's pretty much like a letter of intent or memorandum of understanding (if you're familiar with those kinds of documents).

Your term sheet gives both you and your investor the opportunity to:

- focus on the key issues
- avoid any misunderstandings
- identify any major issues

– before you start the more time-intensive and expensive work of doing due diligence and the full legal documents.

Usually, experienced lead investors provide you with the term sheet, but otherwise you can ask your lawyer to draft the initial document for you – which can be helpful, as you then take control in leading the negotiations and can set out terms that are most favourable to you.

A term sheet doesn't legally bind you into doing the investment deal itself, although once signed, it can be a little tricky to renegotiate. However, some terms of the term sheet will be legally binding, as follows.

Exclusivity period

If the investor insists on this (which VCs often do), it means you can't shop your deal around once the term sheet is signed.

Confidentiality

This is helpful, as it allows you to disclose more information to the investor in confidence, once your term sheet is signed. Note that it means you need to keep the proposed deal outlined in the term sheet confidential, too.

Fees and expenses

Usually, it's made clear in the term sheet that each party is responsible for their own fees and expenses (legal, accounting, etc.) incurred prior to closing the full investment deal.

Conduct of the business

This term is about making sure you keep running the business properly once the term sheet is signed, and don't just jack it all in before the full investment deal is agreed.

Understand deal terms

Let's look in more detail at the main terms that are likely to be covered in your term sheet for a typical equity investment deal.

(Please note these are based on UK investment deal terms. There may be differences in your local legal jurisdiction, if you're raising outside the UK: it's important to get advice from your lawyer on this.)

Ownership

Valuation and share allocation

This outlines:

- who is participating in the round
- how much they're investing
- what they're paying per share
- the type of shares – e.g. Ordinary, which have standard rights, or Preference, which can have extra rights.

Typically, in the UK these would be Ordinary shares, so the investor can qualify for SEIS/EIS (see Chapter 6).

Option pools

This sets aside the pool of shares which will be available for employees in the future. It's a great way to incentivise staff, and investors like to see this scheme in place. Typically, an option pool of around 15 per cent is set aside: it's better for you if this is calculated post-investment, as your shares then won't be diluted as much.

Share price calculation

This outlines whether the price per share is calculated:

- using the pre-money or post-money valuation (see Step 2)
- based on 'issued' share capital – i.e. the shares you've already given out
- based on 'fully diluted' share capital – which also includes the share options you've set aside.

It's more founder-friendly to agree to calculate this on issued shares post-investment, as you'll get a higher share price.

Founder loans

This outlines how any money you've put into the business as a director's loan will be dealt with and paid back, once certain conditions are met: e.g. the business reaching profitability or other KPIs, or converted into equity.

Founder share vesting

This details whether:

- your shares will vest – i.e. be issued or granted over a period: for example, three or four years
- they vest monthly or quarterly
- there is an initial 'cliff' period – meaning that no shares are issued for, as an example, the first year of the agreement. This is designed to prevent you from leaving the business too soon.

Two-thirds of investment deals include these terms, so it's pretty standard. It's also standard for a 'Good Leaver/Bad Leaver' clause to be included, which is designed to prevent you from being issued shares if you're fired for wrongdoing.

Founder salary

If you're raising a round of more than £150,000, then you certainly should be negotiating proper compensation as a valued resource within the company. Consider what it might cost to recruit a replacement for your role, and how much remuneration you genuinely need to make your life work.

As a benchmark, research shows that the average founders' salary is £25,000 when a company is valued at £2 million, rising to £52,000 on a £4 million valuation, and £80,000 at £6 million valuation.[1]

Pre-emption

At every funding round, existing shareholders are diluted and the percentage of the company they own is reduced, because new shares are issued to give to new investors.

To avoid being diluted, current shareholders usually have the option to invest in the company and buy additional shares on a pro-rata basis, prior to shares being made available to external shareholders. This is called 'pre-emption rights'.

Anti-dilution

Anti-dilution rights protect investors with Preference shares (if you have them) from losing ownership and influence, if you do a further fundraising round at a lower valuation than in previous financing rounds (a down-round). It means that they won't get diluted as much as those with Ordinary shares.

Dividends

Dividends are when the profits of the business are paid out to shareholders. Most term sheets mention dividends, but for start-ups this is usually pointless because the objective is to grow and exit the business, rather than paying out profits.

Control

Board seats

Your board of directors governs your company, and agrees and signs off on strategic company decisions, including:

- long-term vision
- hiring and firing key staff members
- major business changes

– so it's important to get the structure and appointments right.

Usually, a three- or five-person board is large enough for an early-stage start-up. Major investors typically want a board seat, so you can expect to allocate one or two places to them.

It's helpful to have an odd number on your board so you can avoid split decisions, and usual to have a structure that gives equal weighting to founders and investors – plus someone independent and trusted by both sides whom you can appoint as chair.

Investor consent

This is the right for investors to veto certain key decisions, including:

- payments and salaries over a certain amount
- taking on debt
- issuing shares
- mergers and acquisitions
- key hires
- changing the company name
- selling or winding up the company.

It's reasonable to expect major investors to have sign-off on these issues.

Information rights

This is the right for the investor (usually one that owns a minimum amount of shares) to have access to certain company information following the investment, such as key performance metrics and financials. Again, this is normal and reasonable.

Exit

Participation rights

This details how much money investors and preference shareholders receive before everyone else when you sell your company, to protect them from losing all their money if it doesn't do well.

The most standard liquidation preference is 1x invested capital: i.e. investors get 100 per cent of their money back before anyone else gets a penny. Usually, there is an option for Preference shareholders to convert their shares into Ordinary shares, then receive cash according to their percentage ownership in the company. They also might be granted a percentage of any proceeds in an exit, on top of the return of their investment.

Drag-along

Drag-along rights means that if someone offers to buy your company and a specified minimum percentage of shareholders want to go ahead, then all shareholders must sell at that price. This stops you being held hostage by a few shareholders who refuse to sell.

A typical drag-along is 75 per cent, which means three-quarters of shareholders need to vote to sell the business on behalf of all shareholders.

Tag-along

Looking at things the other way around, the tag-along clause protects minority shareholders. In the event of an exit share sale by a majority shareholder, tag-along extends the sales right to other shareholders, so that they also can sell their shares at the same price as the majority shareholder, if they want.

Warranties

These are promises you make to your investors about the important things they would expect you to disclose. For example, that:

- the business isn't being sued
- you own all the intellectual property
- your information about your customer database is correct, etc.

The warranties come into effect if a founder breaks the terms in the investment agreement, or fails to disclose some of the things above which might affect an investor's willingness to invest.

Usually, there will be:

- a liability cap – a maximum amount that you would be on the hook for, generally equal to your annual salary
- a liability floor – a minimum amount they would bother pursuing, of around £10,000.

Negotiate your deal

It's important not to blindly accept the terms that are put in front of you without negotiating them to your advantage. You owe it to yourself, your business and the customers you serve to ensure your investment deal is the best you can get, so you can build real long-term value.

When it comes to negotiation, you have more power than you think! You might be surprised to learn that investors expect you to negotiate: if you don't, you could be perceived as a push-over – and that's not how you want to kick off this new business relationship.

Do bear in mind that you're probably going to be in a relationship with your investors for quite a long time – maybe even 10 years – so how you handle discussions is important. Your conduct will reflect on you and your business, and you'll want to maintain their trust and operate with integrity at all times, as you're still being assessed by investors during the deal-closing process.

Of course, investors will be looking to protect their own interests too, and they tend to be savvy and experienced negotiators – but equally, they aren't there to try and get one over on you. The investment ecosystem is small, and reputations are important. Investors want to be known as being fair and good to work with; plus they want the deal to work for you, so you're incentivised to build value in the business and generate the exit they're seeking.

Consider all the terms of a deal, not just valuation: how the business will be run as you scale it, and what happens on exit, are just as important. There are many high-profile horror stories of founders who have been booted out of their own companies, because the deals they negotiated ultimately left them with no control over their own ventures – which is the last thing you want.

The terms you set on this round can set a precedent for later funding rounds, so it's important to get this right.

Here are a few things to think about when it comes to negotiation.

See both sides

Make sure you fully evaluate the other side's interests, as well as your own. If you understand what value your investor is looking for, what they care about, worry about and hope for, you can bring something to the table which has value for them.

This can be a great source of power when you're negotiating your deal.

Manage timescales

It really shouldn't take more than a couple of weeks to get your deal agreed.

Be as responsive as possible so as not to cause unnecessary delays, demonstrate how professional you are, and instil trust. Try not to go back and forth too many times: gather up all your questions and proposed amendments and deal with them in a new draft, rather than pinging minor changes across without thought.

Consider what really matters

Not all the elements of a term sheet are equally important, so figure out what is critical for you to negotiate and what matters less. Prioritise your non-negotiables, so that you know what you will really fight for, and where you might be more prepared to concede.

You must be able to articulate your needs, but also be flexible where you can (and if it makes sense to), so you can get the deal done without arguing over every little thing.

Do your research

Contact other companies in the investor's portfolio to find out:

- what was negotiable
- why they made the choices they did
- what the impact of the deal was afterwards.

This is a good opportunity to do your own final due diligence on your investors, by asking their portfolio founders whether they would recommend your investor.

It's valuable to get professional advice when you're negotiating your term sheet, to make sure you structure your deal in the best way and avoid issues down the line.

> **Remember: sign nothing unless you completely understand it.**

Don't forget, you haven't done the deal just because you have a signed term sheet. The full, deep, due diligence process starts now. Be open and honest with your investors in your information-sharing, remembering they'll be your partners in this business – not the enemy!

Once this is complete to your investor's satisfaction, both parties can move on to finalising the deal paperwork.

Complete the legal paperwork

Your lawyers will take the term sheet to create all the long-form legal documents required to get the deal done. You must agree and sign all of this paperwork before your deal goes through.

Here is a standard list for an early-stage UK investment deal, so you can get a sense of what's involved (again, this may differ if you are raising outside of the UK, so do make sure you seek professional advice from your lawyer).

Long-form legal documents

- Updated Articles of Incorporation – a formal document that shows all the key information about a company, including name, address and shares.
- Updated Capitalisation Table (Cap Table) – the table that shows who the shareholders of your business are, how many shares they each own, and the value of that equity in each investment round.
- Shareholders and Subscription Agreement – which details the investment deal itself.
- Intellectual Property Assignment Agreement – if intellectual property is to be transferred from individuals to the company.
- Employment and Service Agreements – for all team members.
- Disclosure Letter – detailing all the terms, conditions, assets, risks and liabilities associated with the investment deal.

- Representations and Warranties document – this provides indemnity if the assertions made in the Disclosure Letter are found to be untrue.
- Minutes of a board meeting – this must be held to approve funding and share issue.
- Shareholders' Resolution proposal – this details the investment deal, to be signed off by all shareholders.

The lawyers will be responsible for preparing and issuing all the documents to the relevant parties for countersignature. They will ensure that investments are deposited in an escrow account (ringfenced for you, the client), then paid out to you once the deal is done.

Following the deal, your lawyers will support you to:

- create, sign and issue Shareholder Certificates – so that each investor has an official record of their shareholding
- update your Company Share Register – which is held by the government to track your shares and who owns them
- file a SH01 form with Companies House – to inform them that new shares have been allotted
- complete and send SEIS/EIS post-completion forms to HMRC – with details of new shareholders. Once compliance certificates have been issued to the company by HMRC, SEIS/EIS certificates are issued to individual shareholders.

It can take anything from two weeks to a couple of months until completion and the money hitting your bank account, depending on the complexity of your deal and the efficiency of all the lawyers and parties involved. This period can feel quite stressful, while you wait for all the pieces of the puzzle to finally fall into place.

Time to celebrate!

Last but not least: get your celebration drinks on ice, because once everything is signed, you will finally see that money coming into your business bank account, and be ready to start putting all your exciting growth plans in place.

There really is no better feeling.

Make sure you take time to celebrate with your team and everyone who has supported you along the way. And get ready for the next stage of your entrepreneurial journey!

Action steps

1. Establish clear timelines for your campaign and communicate them to investors. Maintain regular contact with investors throughout the process of completing and closing your deal.
2. Tell new potential investors about any lead investment you've secured, and leverage the network of committed investors to find even more connections.
3. Negotiate and agree your term sheet first, to capture key elements of the deal. Prioritise non-negotiables, and ensure you understand everything to which you are agreeing.
4. Do your own due diligence on investors by speaking with other founders they've backed, to see what it's like to work with them.
5. Work with lawyers experienced in venture transactions to execute your deal for you – there is a lot of paperwork involved.
6. Think about how you'll celebrate when your deal is done, so that you properly recognise and reward both yourself and

those who've helped you along the way in this momentous achievement.

Epilogue

I truly hope you've found this book a useful step-by-step resource to raising investment – and that the stories you've heard from the female founders who have blazed the trail have inspired you to reach for great things!

By applying these principles and approach, you now have the very best chance of a successful equity fundraise.

As you go forth on your journey to grow, fund and scale your start-up, I encourage you to lift others up along the way – particularly those under-represented founders who might be facing extra challenges in navigating the world of investment. Together we are stronger: our positive, open action moves us ever nearer to closing the gender funding gap, and enabling a greater number of incredible women to lead the businesses of the future.

In time, when you have your own story of fundraising success to share, I'd love to hear from you. Nothing excites me more than seeing female founders fly and making a real difference in the world.

Wishing you all the very best!

Julia

juliaelliottbrown@enterthearena.co.uk
www.juliaelliottbrown.com   *www.enterthearena.co.uk*

Notes

Introduction

1 H. Skingle, L. Wilson, H. Whorwood, D. Robinson, F. Hyde and A. Williams (2021) 'The deal 2021', Beauhurst. Available at: *www.beauhurst.com/research/the-deal*, accessed 30 May 2022; K. Nicol-Schwartz (2021) 'Female founders received just 1% of funding in CEE region in 2020', *Sifted*, 24 March. Available at: *https://sifted.eu/articles/female-founded-startups-cee*, accessed 30 May 2022; G. Teare (2020) 'Global VC funding to female founders dropped dramatically this year', *Crunchbase News*, 21 December. Available at: *https://news.crunchbase.com/venture/global-vc-funding-to-female-founders/*, accessed 30 May 2022.

2 HSBC Private Banking (2019) 'She's the business: Supporting entrepreneurial spirit'. Available at: *https://tinyurl.com/5rpzhpb8*, accessed 30 May 2022.

3 NatWest (2021) 'The Alison Rose review', 15 March. Available at: *https://natwestbusinesshub.com/articles/rosereview*, accessed 30 May 2022.

Chapter 2

1 J. Zenger and J. Folkman (2019) 'Research: Women score higher than men in most leadership skills', *Harvard Business Review*, 25 June. Available at: *https://hbr.org/2019/06/research-women-score-higher-than-men-in-most-leadership-skills*, accessed 30 May 2022.

2 C. West and G. Sundaramurthy (2019) 'Startups with at least 1 female founder hire 2.5x more women', Kauffman Fellows, 17 October. Available at: *www.kauffmanfellows.org/journal_posts/female_founders_hire_more_women*, accessed 30 May 2022.

3 V. Hunt, L. Yee, S. Prince and S. Dixon-Fyle (2018) 'Delivering through diversity', McKinsey & Company, 18 January. Available at: *www.mckinsey.com/business-functions/people-and-organizational-performance/our-insights/delivering-through-diversity*, accessed 30 May 2022.

4 A. Sijamic Wahid (2019) 'The effects and the mechanisms of board gender diversity: Evidence from financial manipulation', *Journal of Business Ethics* 159: 705–725. Available at: *https://link.springer.com/article/10.1007/s10551-018-3785-6*, accessed 30 May 2022.

5 R. Soares, C. Marquis and M. Lee (2011) 'Gender and corporate social responsibility: It's a matter of sustainability', *Catalyst*. Available at: *www.catalyst.org/wp-content/uploads/2019/01/gender_and_corporate_social_responsibility.pdf*, accessed 30 May 2022.

6 First Round (2015) '10-year project'. Available at: *http://10years.firstround.com*, accessed 30 May 2022.

7 Beauhurst (2017) 'Female founders: The data on women in business', 5 September. Available at: *www.beauhurst.com/blog/female-founders-data-women-business*, accessed 30 May 2022.

8 K. Abouzahr, M. Krentz, J. Harthorne and F. Brooks Taplett (2018) 'Why women-owned startups are a better bet', BCG, 6 June. Available at: *www.bcg.com/en-us/publications/2018/why-women-owned-startups-are-better-bet*, accessed 30 May 2022.

9 A. Rose (2019) 'The Alison Rose review of female entrepreneurship'. Available at: *https://assets.publishing.service.gov.uk/government/uploads/system/uploads/attachment_data/file/784324/RoseReview_Digital_FINAL.PDF*, accessed 30 May 2022.

10 Rose, 'The Alison Rose review of female entrepreneurship'.

11 NatWest (2021) 'The Alison Rose review', 15 March. Available at: *https://natwestbusinesshub.com/articles/rosereview*, accessed 30 May 2022.

12 HM Treasury (2021) 'Investing in women code: Annual progress report 2021', April. Available at: *https://assets.publishing.service.gov.uk/government/uploads/system/uploads/attachment_data/file/978515/2020_Annual_Investing_in_Women_Code_report_FINAL.pdf*, accessed 30 May 2022.

13 British Business Bank (2019) 'UK VC and female founders report'. Available at: *https://www.british-business-bank.co.uk/uk-vc-female-founders-report*, accessed 30 May 2022.

14 K. Clark (2018) 'Female founders have brought in just 2.2% of US VC this year (yes, again)', *TechCrunch*, 4 November. Available at: *https://techcrunch.com/2018/11/04/female-founders-have-brought-in-just-2-2-of-us-vc-this-year-yes-again*, accessed 30 May 2022.

15 M. Malmstrom, J. Johansson and J. Wincent (2017) 'We recorded VCs' conversations and analyzed how differently they talk about female entrepreneurs', *Harvard Business Review*, 17 May. Available at: *https://hbr.org/2017/05/we-recorded-vcs-conversations-and-analyzed-how-differently-they-talk-about-female-entrepreneurs*, accessed 30 May 2022.

16 D. Kanze, L. Huang, M.A. Conley and E. Tory Higgins (2017) 'Male and female entrepreneurs get asked different questions by VCs – and it affects how much funding they get', *Harvard Business Review*, 27 June. Available at: *https://hbr.org/2017/06/male-and-female-entrepreneurs-get-asked-different-questions-by-vcs-and-it-affects-how-much-funding-they-get*, accessed 30 May 2022.

17 A. Weiland, D. Pocull and M. Goodwin (2018) 'State of startups 2018', First Round. Available at: *http://stateofstartups.firstround.com/2018/#parents-at-work*, accessed 30 May 2022.

18 A. Wood Brooks, L. Huang, S. Wood Kearney and F.E. Murray (2014) 'Investors prefer entrepreneurial ventures pitched by attractive men', *PNAS* 111(12): 4427–4431. Available at: *www.pnas.org/content/111/12/4427*, accessed 30 May 2022.

19 Wood Brooks et al, 'Investors prefer entrepreneurial ventures pitched by attractive men'.

20 R. Solnit (2014) *Men Explain Things to Me*, Haymarket.

21 Rose, 'The Alison Rose review of female entrepreneurship'.

22 HM Treasury, 'Investing In women code: Annual progress report 2021'.

23 Rose, 'The Alison Rose review of female entrepreneurship'.

24 H. Skingle, L. Wilson, H. Whorwood, D. Robinson, F. Hyde and A. Williams (2021) 'The deal 2021', Beauhurst. Available at: *www.beauhurst.com/research/the-deal*, accessed 30 May 2022.

25 Beauhurst, 'Female founders: the data on women in business'.

Chapter 3

1 D. Gage (2012) 'The venture capital secret: 3 out of 4 start-ups fail', *Wall Street Journal*, 20 September. Available at: *www.wsj.com/articles/SB10000872396390443720204578004980476429190*, accessed 30 May 2022.

2 M. Flint (2020) 'Cash flow: The reason 82% of small businesses fail', *Preferred CFO*, 8 June. Available at: *www.preferredcfo.com/cash-flow-reason-small-businesses-fail*, accessed 30 May 2022.

Chapter 4

1 S. Marsh (2017) 'Girls as young as seven in UK boxed in by gender stereotyping', *The Guardian*, 21 September. Available at: *www.theguardian.com/world/2017/sep/21/girls-seven-uk-boxed-in-by-gender-stereotyping-equality*, accessed 30 May 2022.

2 R. Adams, N. McIntyre and S. Weale (2019) 'GCSE results: Girls fare better than boys under more rigorous courses', *The Guardian*, 22 August. Available at: *www.theguardian.com/education/2019/aug/22/gcse-results-more-rigorous-courses-appear-to-benefit-girls*, accessed 30 May 2022.

3 Organisation for Economic Cooperation and Development (OECD) (2018) 'Bridging the gender digital divide: Include, upskill, innovate'. Available at: *www.oecd.org/internet/bridging-the-digital-gender-divide.pdf*, accessed 30 May 2022.

4 World Economic Forum (2018) 'The global gender gap report'. Available at: *www3.weforum.org/docs/WEF_GGGR_2018.pdf*, accessed 30 May 2022.

5 J. Zenger and J. Folkman (2019) 'Research: Women score higher than men in most leadership skills', *Harvard Business Review*, 25 June. Available at: *https://hbr.org/2019/06/research-women-score-higher-than-men-in-most-leadership-skills*, accessed 30 May 2022.

6 A. Fels (2004) 'Do women lack ambition?', *Harvard Business Review*, April. Available at: *https://hbr.org/2004/04/do-women-lack-ambition*, accessed 30 May 2022.

7 Z. Bernard (2018) 'The idea that most successful start-up founders are in their twenties is a myth – the average entrepreneur is much older', *Business Insider*, 24 April. Available at: *www.businessinsider.com/young-startup-founder-myth-average-age-of-entrepreneurs-42-mit-study-2018-4*, accessed 30 May 2022.

8 S. Dumitriu (2019) 'Future founders', The Entrepreneurs Network, 12 August. Available at: *www.tenentrepreneurs.org/research/future-founders-understanding-the-next-generation-of-entrepreneurs*, accessed 30 May 2022.

9 C. Leitch, F. Welter and C. Henry (2018) 'Women entrepreneurs' financing revisited: Taking stock and looking forward', *International Journal of Entrepreneurial Finance* 20(2): 103–114. Available at: *www.tandfonline.com/doi/full/10.1080/13691066.2018.1418624*, accessed 30 May 2022.

10 L.M. Giurge, A.V. Whillans and A. Yemiscigil (2021) 'A multicountry perspective on gender difference in time use during Covid-19', *PNAS* 118(12). Available at: *www.pnas.org/content/118/12/e2018494118*, accessed 30 May 2022.

11 A. Rose (2019) 'The Alison Rose review of female entrepreneurship'. Available at: *https://assets.publishing.service.gov.uk/government/uploads/system/uploads/attachment_data/file/784324/RoseReview_Digital_FINAL.PDF*, accessed 30 May 2022.

Chapter 5

1 Beauhurst (2019) 'We tracked every startup that raised venture capital in 2011', 23 May. Available at: *www.beauhurst.com/blog/startups-of-yesteryear-2019-update*, accessed 30 May 2022.

Chapter 6

1 C. Leitch, F. Welter and C. Henry (2018) 'Women entrepreneurs' financing revisited: Taking stock and looking forward', *International Journal of Entrepreneurial Finance* 20(2): 103–114. Available at: *www.tandfonline.com/doi/full/10.1080/13691066.2018.1418624*, accessed 30 May 2022.

2 DocSend Start-up Index (2021) 'The seed round in 2020–21: Make or break moment for founders'. Available at: *https://docsend.com/view/b3ax35s2jspk5xxp*, accessed 30 May 2022.

3 H. Skingle, A. Scott and E. Halmari (2019) 'Female entrepreneurs: Gender diversity across the UK's high-growth ecosystem', Beauhurst. Available at: *www.beauhurst.com/research/female-entrepreneurs*, accessed 30 May 2022.

4 H. Skingle, H. Whorwood, A. Scott, J. Hawkins and D. Robinson (2019) 'The deal: Equity investment in the UK 2019', Beauhurst. Available at: *www.beauhurst.com/wp-content/uploads/2020/02/The-Deal-2019_WEB.pdf*, accessed 30 May 2022.

5 A. Rose (2019) 'How to value your company and how much equity to give away', Seed Legals, 23 October. Available at: *https://seedlegals.com/resources/how-to-value-your-company*, accessed 30 May 2022; B. McClure (2021) 'Valuing startup ventures', Investopedia, 30 July. Available at: *www.investopedia.com/articles/financial-theory/11/valuing-startup-ventures.asp*, accessed 30 May 2022.

6 M. Wright, M. Hart and K. Fu (2015) 'A nation of angels: Assessing the impact of angel investing across the UK', Enterprise Research, January. Available at: *www.enterpriseresearch.ac.uk/wp-content/uploads/2015/01/ERC-Angels-Report..pdf*, accessed 30 May 2022.

Chapter 7

1 DocSend Start-up Index (2021) 'The seed round in 2020–21: Make or break moment for founders'. Available at: *https://docsend.com/view/b3ax35s2jspk5xxp*, accessed 30 May 2022.

Chapter 8

1 A. Rose (2020) 'SeedLegals funding rounds stats', Seed Legals, 13 February. Available at: *https://seedlegals.com/resources/seedlegals-funding-round-stats*, accessed 30 May 2022.

2 A. Cremades (2019) 'How startup accelerators work', *Forbes*, 10 January. Available at: *www.forbes.com/sites/alejandrocremades/2019/01/10/how-startup-accelerators-work*, accessed 30 May 2022.

3 Social Innovation Monitor (2019) 'Full report on the impact of incubators/accelerators in the UK'. Available at: *https://socialinnovationmonitor.com/en/uk-incubators*, accessed 30 May 2022; J. Wilson (2022) 'How do startup accelerators work?', Silicon Valley Bank. Available at: *https://www.svb.com/startup-insights/startup-growth/how-do-startup-accelerators-work#*, accessed 30 May 2022.

4 Henry Whorwood (2018) 'Accelerating the UK', Beauhurst, 17 October. Available at: *https://www.beauhurst.com/accelerating-the-uk-report/#sector*, accessed 30 May 2022.

5 Whorwood, 'Accelerating the UK'.

6 HM Treasury (2021) 'Investing in women code: Annual Progress Report 2021', April. Available at: *https://assets.publishing.service.gov.uk/government/uploads/system/uploads/attachment_data/file/978515/2020_Annual_Investing_in_Women_Code_report_FINAL.pdf*, accessed 30 May 2022.

7 British Business Bank (2018) 'The UK business angels market report'. Available at: *www.british-business-bank.co.uk/wp-content/uploads/2018/06/Business-Angel-Reportweb.pdf*, accessed 30 May 2022.

8 British Business Bank, 'The UK business angels market report'.

9 SVB Capital and Campden Wealth (2020) 'Family offices investing in venture capital 2020', Silicon Valley Bank, January. Available at: *www.svb.com/globalassets/library/managedassets/pdfs/fos-in-vc-2020_18aug.pdf*, accessed 30 May 2022.

10 SVB Capital and Campden Wealth, 'Family offices investing in venture capital 2020.

11 K. Darrah (2019) 'Family office investment into European startups jumps fivefold', *Sifted*, 3 December. Available at: *https://sifted.eu/articles/investment-vc-wealth-dealroom*, accessed 30 May 2022.

12 British Business Bank (2019) 'UK VC and female founders report'. Available at: *https://www.british-business-bank.co.uk/uk-vc-female-founders-report*, accessed 30 May 2022.

13 A. Scott (2019) 'Female entrepreneurs', Newable and Beauhurst. Available at: *https://newable.co.uk/wp-content/uploads/2019/12/Female-Entrepreneurs-2019-WEB.pdf*, accessed 30 May 2022.

14 First Round (2019) 'State of startups 2019'. Available at: *https://stateofstartups2019.firstround.com*, accessed 30 May 2022.

15 A. Rose (2019) 'The Alison Rose review of female entrepreneurship'. Available at: *https://assets.publishing.service.gov.uk/government/uploads/system/uploads/attachment_data/file/784324/RoseReview_Digital_FINAL.PDF*, accessed 30 May 2022.

16 First Round (2018) 'State of startups: Fundraising'. Available at: *http://stateofstartups.firstround.com/2018/#fundraising*, accessed 30 May 2022.

Chapter 9

1 D. Kanze, L. Huang, M.A. Conley and E. Tory Higgins (2017) 'Male and female entrepreneurs get asked different questions by VCs – and it affects how much funding they get', *Harvard Business Review*, 27 June. Available at: *https://hbr.org/2017/06/male-and-female-entrepreneurs-get-asked-different-questions-by-vcs-and-it-affects-how-much-funding-they-get*, accessed 30 May 2022.

Chapter 10

1 Seedrs (2019) 'How much salary should a founder take?' Available at: *www.seedrs.com/academy/how-much-salary-should-a-founder-take*, accessed 30 May 2022.

Further resources

Investability Scorecard

To assess your potential to raise investment and understand your strengths and weaknesses in each of the 5 Steps to Fundraising, complete my free, confidential test for female founders.

This reveals your personal strengths and weaknesses and delivers practical, actionable tips to improve your results and help you secure the funding you need:

Company – is your business likely to be attractive to investors?

Commercials – are you confident on your forecasts, raise amount and valuation?

Communication – can you clearly articulate your investment narrative?

Connection – are you able to reach out to and attract the right investors?

Commitment – can you secure backing from investors and negotiate a good deal?

To take the test, go to *www.enterthearena.co.uk/investability-scorecard*

It takes about 10 minutes to answer the 40 questions in the test. You'll instantly receive a report with your unique score, showing where you stand against the competition and giving you tips to improve your chances of raising investment.

Podcast

In my podcast, *Fundraising Stories With Female Founders*, I showcase even more inspirational interviews with female founders who share their honest experiences of fundraising – the highs, the lows, the challenges and top tips for how to be successful.

You can watch the original video interviews, along with the audio at *www.enterthearena.co.uk/fundraising-stories*

Spotify: *https://open.spotify.com/show/002pNa2BqPaxowewAjSBOF*

Apple Podcasts: *https://podcasts.apple.com/gb/podcast/fundraising-stories-with-female-founders/id1448466219*

The podcast is also available on all other major podcast platforms.

Coaching programmes: Enter The Arena

Enter The Arena provides female founders with the skills and confidence to scale your business. Our programmes shortcut the heartache of juggling a thriving business operation while building growth.

Whether it's getting started with raising capital or scaling to exit, we meet you where you are and bring the know-how to support your business journey, helping you to deliver long-term value.

Visit: *www.enterthearena.co.uk*

Enter The Arena's female founder community

It would be my pleasure to invite you to join Enter The Arena's community of high-growth female founders, in our private Facebook group at: *www.facebook.com/groups/femalefoundersfly*

Please request membership and tell us about your business and your fundraising journey as part of your application.

Alternative sources of funding

These are a few of the funding resources I personally recommend (please note it's by no means an exhaustive list, and UK-focused).

Rewards-based crowdfunding
Crowdfunder: *www.crowdfunder.co.uk*

Indigogo: *https://grow.indiegogo.com*

Kickstarter: *www.kickstarter.com*

Grants
Eileen Fisher Women-owned Business Grant:
www.eileenfisher.com/social-consciousness/grants-overview

Grant Tree: *https://granttree.co.uk*

Innovate UK: *www.innovateukedge.ukri.org*

Loans
British Business Bank start-up loan: *www.startuploans.co.uk*

Coralus: *https://sheeo.world*

Funding Circle business loans: *www.fundingcircle.com*

Virgin start-up loans: *www.virginstartup.org/start-up-loans*

R&D tax credits

HMRC: *www.gov.uk/guidance/corporation-tax-research-and-development-rd-relief*

Marketing funding

ClearCo: *https://clear.co*

Pipe: *https://pipe.com*

Wayflyer: *www.wayflyer.com*

Marketing resources

Cascade vision statement examples: *www.cascade.app/blog/examples-good-vision-statements*

Wix vision statement examples: *www.wix.com/blog/2021/03/vision-statement*

Financial and legal support

These are some of the organisations that I partner with in the UK.

Accounting and finance

Ask The Boss: *www.ask-the-boss.co.uk*

Newton's Theory: *www.newtonstheory.com*

Tiny CFO: *www.tinycfo.com*

Legal support

Illume: *https://illumelegal.co.uk*

Seed Legals: *https://seedlegals.com*

Financial modelling tools

Canaree: *www.canaree.co*

Graphite free templates:
https://graphitefinancial.com/open-source-financial-model

ProForma start-up financial model:
www.startupfinancialmodel.com

Start-up Falcon valuation tool: *https://startupfalcon.com*

UK SEIS/EIS Investment scheme
HMRC Advanced Assurance application:
www.gov.uk/guidance/venture-capital-schemes-apply-for-advance-assurance

HMRC schemes overview: *www.gov.uk/topic/business-tax/investment-schemes*

Female-focused entrepreneurial networks

Some great networks and initiatives you might want to consider:

AllBright: *www.allbrightcollective.com*

Cartier Women's Initiative: *www.cartierwomensinitiative.com*

Enterprise Nation Entrepreneurial Women:
www.enterprisenation.com/entrepreneurialwomen

Everywoman Self-Made Entrepreneurs Hub:
www.everywoman-selfmade.com

EY Entrepreneurial Winning Women: *www.ey.com/en_us/entrepreneurial-winning-women-north-america*

Financial Alliance for Women:
https://financialallianceforwomen.org

Founder Institute Female Founder Initiative: *www.female-founderinitiative.com*

Global Invest Her: *www.globalinvesther.com*

Goldman Sachs 10,000 Women: *www.goldmansachs.com/citizenship/10000women*

Hatch: *https://hatchenterprise.org*

HSBC Roar: *http://promo.allbrightcollective.com/partnership/hsbc/roar*

iFundWomen: *https://ifundwomen.com*

Meta #SheMeansBusiness: *www.facebook.com/business/shemeansbusiness*

Sistr: *www.sistrapp.com*

Springboard Enterprises: *https://sb.co*

The Entrepreneurs Network Female Founders' Forum: *www.tenentrepreneurs.org/aboutfff*

The Women's Chapter: *https://womenschapter.com*

Women Entrepreneurs Finance Initiative (We-Fi): *https://we-fi.org*

Women's Venture Fund: *https://womensventurefund.org*

Investors

Female-focused investors

For an up-to-date list of some of the better-known funds investing in female founders, go to: *www.enterthearena.co.uk/investors-in-female-founders*

Family offices

Family Office Hub: *https://familyofficehub.io/product/list-of-largest-single-family-offices-uk-investment-details-database*

Crowdfunding platforms

Crowdcube: *www.crowdcube.com*

Money Crashers US crowdfunding platforms: *www.moneycrashers.com/equity-crowdfunding-sites-investors-entrepreneurs*

Seedrs: *www.seedrs.com*

Pitch events

To learn more about specific pitch events that are held to showcase female founder led businesses, go to: *www.enterthearena.co.uk/female-founder-pitch-events*

Diversity initiatives

Some key initiatives in the UK:

Diversity VC: *https://diversity.vc*

The Gender Index: *www.thegenderindex.co.uk*

The UK Business Angels Association (UKBAA) Angel Investment in Diversity: Best Practice Guidance: *www.ukbaa.org.uk/wp-content/uploads/2021/12/diversityguidance.pdf*

Inspirational books

Brené Brown (2015) *Daring Greatly: How the Courage to Be Vulnerable Transforms the Way We Live, Love, Parent, and Lead*, Penguin Life.

Robert Cialdini (2007) *Influence: The Psychology of Persuasion*, HarperBusiness.

Caroline Criado Perez (2019) *Invisible Women: Exposing Data Bias in a World Designed for Men*, Vintage.

Jane Cunningham and Philippa Roberts (2021) *Brandsplaining: Why Marketing is (Still) Sexist and How to Fix It*, Penguin Business.

Michael Hayman and Nick Giles (2015) *Mission: How the Best in Business Break Through*, Portfolio Penguin.

Gay Hendricks (2010) *The Big Leap: Conquer Your Hidden Fear and Take Life to the Next Level*, HarperOne.

Reid Hoffman and Chris Yeh (2018) *Blitzscaling: The Lightning-Fast Path to Building Massively Valuable Companies*, HarperCollins.

Gary Keller and Jay Papasan (2014) *The One Thing: The Surprisingly Simple Truth Behind Extraordinary Results*, John Murray Learning.

Helen Lewis (2020) *Difficult Women: A History of Feminism in 11 Fights*, Jonathan Cape.

Eric Ries (2011) *The Lean Startup: How Constant Innovation Creates Radically Successful Businesses*, Portfolio Penguin.

Acknowledgements

First, I'd like to give huge thanks to all the incredible female founders who shared their stories and agreed to participate in this book: you are an absolute inspiration, and I feel very lucky to know you all!

To fellow authors Nicola Cook, Jane Cunningham, Philippa Roberts and Charly Lester, who gave some great advice on how to get this done; and a nod to Michael Hayman MBE, who gave me the advice not to write it (I hope you were wrong!).

My wonderful editor, Lisa Cordaro, who has shaped this into the helpful guide it was always meant to be: her insights and experience have been invaluable.

And my small but passionate and dedicated team at Enter The Arena.

Big shout out to Mark Esiri at Venrex, who always reassured me that I would be absolutely fine, even though there were moments where I wasn't sure I'd be able to pick myself up again. Geeta Sidhu-Robb, who gave me the courage to follow my passion in starting Enter The Arena. My sage business coach, Dilys Greenwood, who has supported me in so many ways through the years, asking me those difficult questions and challenging me to think differently.

Thank you to all my connections in the start-up and investment industry, who share my mission of achieving gender parity in the world of investment, and continually reassured me how much this book is needed: with a particular shout out to fellow female network-builders Michelle de Klerk, Claire Dodds, Emma Hardcastle and Emma Sayle – you're all amazing.

Finally, to friends and family – in particular, Will and Katy, who have had to listen to me as I laboured and gave birth to the book, with quite a lot of moaning and despair along the way (from me) and warm encouragement (from them).

About the author

Julia Elliott Brown, CEO and Founder of Enter The Arena, is the UK's leading equity fundraising expert and specialist coach, working exclusively with female founders.

With a history of building her own high-growth start-ups across multiple sectors, and having successfully raised millions of pounds in equity finance, Julia has a wealth of expertise in building an investor-ready business. Julia's been there, done that and has the t-shirt (and scars) to prove it. Her purpose and passion are to bring her wealth of expertise to support female founders on their own journeys to successful equity fundraising and business growth.

Julia hosts the *Fundraising Stories With Female Founders* podcast, is a seasoned keynote speaker at numerous start-up and fundraising events, and speaks regularly in the press, representing the voice of the female founder and levelling the investment playing field. She is a longstanding judge at the Great British Entrepreneur Awards.

After 25 years in London, Julia now lives on the 'Kent Riviera', a stone's throw from the beach, with her two teenage children and cocker spaniel, Kenny. She's a keen cook, avid wine drinker and loves to sing and dance to gospel, funk and soul music.

Notes